THE WORLD'S CLASSICS

PEER GYNT

HENRIK IBSEN was born in 1828, the son of a Norwegian merchant, who suffered financial setbacks during the boy's childhood, causing him to be apprenticed to an apothecary at the age of fifteen. In 1850 Ibsen came to Christiania (Oslo) with the intention of studying at the university there, but soon abandoned this idea in order to devote himself to writing. His first play, *Catiline*, aroused little interest, but his second, *The Burial Mound*, was staged, and not unsuccessfully. He held posts as producer and resident dramatist in theatres in Bergen and Christiania successively, but his policies in the latter post were severely criticized, and in 1864 he embarked on a long period of self-imposed exile abroad with his wife and their only child, Sigurd. Recognition of Ibsen's true genius came after the publication in 1866 of the dramatic poem *Brand*, and he was at last awarded an annual grant by the Norwegian Parliament to devote himself to writing. From 1868 to 1891 he lived mainly in Dresden, Munich and Rome, and during this period wrote most of the prose plays which established his European reputation. He returned to live in Norway in 1891, and his seventieth birthday was the occasion of national celebrations. His literary career was terminated by a stroke in 1900, and he died on 23 May 1906.

JAMES MCFARLANE, editor of the Oxford Ibsen, is Emeritus Professor of European Literature at the University of East Anglia. His publications include several critical studies of modern European and Scandinavian Literature.

CHRISTOPHER FRY's many plays include *The Lady's Not For Burning* (1949), *A Sleep of Prisoners* (1951), *The Dark is Light Enough* (1954), and *A Yard of Sun* (1970).

JOHAN FILLINGER is a director, actor, and translator and lives in Norway.

Hamsun was born in 1859, the son of a Norwegian merchant who suffered financial reverses during the boy's childhood, causing him to be apprenticed to an shoemaker at the age of fifteen. In 1890 there came to Chicago, Ohio, as a dishwasher, of studying at the university, there, but soon abandoned this idea in order to throw himself to write his first play. Getting across little interest, but this reputation declined. Hamsun was staged, and the unsuccessfully. Hamsun gets a publisher and established himself in literature in the Bergen and Christiania successively, and his policies in the 1880's were severely criticized, and in 1891 he embarked on a long period of self-imposed exile abroad with his wife and their only child. Sigurd. Recognition of Hamsun's true nature came after the publication in 1890 of the dramatic poem *Growth*, and he was at last regarded an important by the Norwegian Parliament to devote himself to writing. From 1891 to 1911 he lived mainly in Denmark, Munich and Munich, and during this period wrote most of the prose plays which established his European reputation. He returned to Norway in 1911 and lived there until his death, was the occasion of national celebration. His literary career was terminated by a stroke in 1952, and he died on 23 May 1962.

JAMES MCFARLANE, editor of the Oxford Ibsen, is also Professor of European Literature in the University of East Anglia. His publications include general studies of modern European and Scandinavian literature.

CHRISTOPHER FRY's plays include *The Lady's Not For Burning* (1949), *A Sleep of Prisoners* (1951), *The Dark is Light Enough* (1954), and *Curtmantle*.

JOHAN BORGEN is a director, actor, and translator and lives in Norway.

THE WORLD'S CLASSICS

═══

HENRIK IBSEN

Peer Gynt
A Dramatic Poem

═══

Translated by
CHRISTOPHER FRY *and* JOHAN FILLINGER

With an introduction by
JAMES McFARLANE

Oxford   New York
OXFORD UNIVERSITY PRESS

Oxford University Press, Walton Street, Oxford OX2 6DP

Oxford New York Toronto
Delhi Bombay Calcutta Madras Karachi
Petaling Jaya Singapore Hong Kong Tokyo
Nairobi Dar es Salaam Cape Town
Melbourne Auckland

and associated companies in
Berlin Ibadan

Oxford is a trade mark of Oxford University Press

Introduction © James McFarlane 1989
Select Bibliography © James McFarlane 1988
Chronology © James McFarlane 1981
Text of Peer Gynt © Christopher Fry and Johan Fillinger 1970
First published as a World's Classics paperback 1989
Reprinted 1992

British Library Cataloguing in Publication Data

Ibsen, Henrik, 1828–1906
Peer Gynt.—(The world's classics)
I. Title II. Fry, Christopher, 1907–
III. Fillinger, Johan
839.8'226

ISBN 0-19-282227-6

Library of Congress Cataloging in Publication Data

Ibsen, Henrik, 1828–1906.
[Peer Gynt, English]
Peer Gynt/Henrik Ibsen; translated by Christopher Fry and Johan Fillinger;
with an introduction by James McFarlane.
p.cm.—(The World's classics)
Translation of: Peer Gynt.
Bibliography: p.
I. Fry, Christopher. II. Fillinger, Johan. III. Title. IV. Series.
839.8'226—dc19   PT8876.A3295 1989   88–31860

ISBN 0-19-282227-6

Printed in Great Britain by
BPCC Hazells Ltd
Aylesbury, Bucks

CONTENTS

INTRODUCTION

Improbably, for a work so assertively Norwegian in its inspiration, *Peer Gynt* was from first to last written under alien Mediterranean skies. No less astonishing, for a piece conceived on such a huge scale, is the fact that it was written, printed and published all within the confines of a single calendar year: 1867. Ibsen began work on it in Rome in January of that year. He warned his publisher that it would be 'a large-scale dramatic poem, the main character of which is to be one of those half-mythological fairy-tale figures in the public domain from the *recent* past'. Act I was complete before the end of February; Act II by the end of March. In May he moved to Ischia, to Casamicciola, where in the torrid heat of the Italian summer, with the thermometer regularly climbing to the high nineties Fahrenheit and beyond, he worked on Act III. During the whole of this period, he was (as William Archer later reported) working 'at very high pressure, amounting to nervous overstrain, ... writing verses all the time, even when asleep or half-awake'. By the beginning of August, the first three acts had been completed; and with supreme confidence (or possibly, as Ibsen himself was later to hint, with great recklessness), he sent off this material to the printer before the last two acts were even properly drafted. Shortly afterwards he moved to Sorrento, where he wrote the fourth and fifth acts, sending the remaining fair copy to his Copenhagen publisher on 18 October. The final stages of the printing process were rushed through at high speed, and the work was published on 14 November 1867.

Within Scandinavia, it was in its book form an immediate commercial success. Practically the whole of the first printing was sold out before publication day. A second printing came out within two weeks of the first. It continued to exert a great appeal to the reading public; and by the end of the century it had reached its eleventh edition.

But whilst in a materialistic sense the public's initial reception of *Peer Gynt* had been heartening, and had contributed greatly to Ibsen's new-found confidence in himself which followed the improvement in his economic circumstances, he awaited with much trepidation the reaction of the heavyweight critics of the day.

When it came, it was devastating. Clemens Petersen, the most influential Danish critic of the time, in a very negative review denied that the work could even properly make claim to be classed as 'poetry'. The influential Georg Brandes, clearly outraged by what he felt were the repulsive crudities of Act IV, dismissed the work as 'neither beautiful nor true', and demanded that Ibsen's practice of 'besmirching human nature' should now cease. A furious Ibsen responded by insisting that the work *was* poetry; and that if it were not judged so, then the whole concept of poetry would have to change to accommodate it.

Peer Gynt marks the last use by Ibsen of verse as a medium of dramatic expression. At the time of its publication, Ibsen was aged 39—the arithmetical mid-point of a life which ended with the author's death at the age of 78 in 1906. This abandonment of verse in order to write 'problem plays' in prose not only represents a turning point in the author's own development as a dramatist but also heralds a wholly new epoch in the history of modern European drama. Ibsen's awareness, following the trauma of the initial critical reception given to *Peer Gynt*, of a new potential within dramatic prose language was a key factor in helping to create a new attitude to dramatic language and in gaining acceptance for the notion of a 'poetry of the theatre' embracing a range of linguistic practices previously neglected or despised. And with it has come the recognition that, paradoxically, the luxuriant fantasy of the verse of *Peer Gynt* held within it the seeds of that spare, sometimes bleak but always (in its own terms) theatrically eloquent dialogue of the later prose plays, and in its train much of what is most characteristic of twentieth-century drama.

The previous year had seen the publication of Ibsen's other great 'dramatic poem', *Brand*; and the essential complementarity of these two works is something which criticism, taking its cue from Ibsen himself, has found it particularly enlightening to explore. Clearly, circumstances imposed on the two works a relationship of special intimacy, making of them in some respects polar opposites, in others matching correlatives. They grew out of a common *raptus* in those first heady years of Ibsen's voluntary exile from Norway, which he left in 1864: 'Can I not ... point to *Brand* and *Peer Gynt* and say "Look, that was like being intoxicated with wine"?' Moreover, although initially quick to inform his pub-

lisher in advance that the new work would 'show no resemblance
to *Brand*', Ibsen often went out of his way in later life to relate
them to the same sources of self-analysis: 'Brand is myself in my
best moments,' he confessed, 'just as I also derived many features
of Peer Gynt ... from self-dissection.'

Ibsen himself advanced the view, in a letter to Edmund Gosse
in 1872, that *Peer Gynt* was *Brand*'s 'opposite' (or 'antithesis', or
'contrary', or 'reversal', or 'counterpart'—the meaning in his
term is multi-layered). Most obviously this relates to the contrast-
ing natures and values of the eponymous heroes: the one unbend-
ing, uncompromising, and sternly dedicated to the principle of
'All or Nothing'; the other unprincipled, opportunist, day-
dreaming and compliant. But, as the Thin Man points out to Peer
in the last act, when it comes to self-portraiture or self-projection
there is no fundamental irreconcilability here:

> Don't forget there are two ways of being yourself...
> You can either show the straightforward picture
> Or else what is called the negative.
> In the latter light and shade are reversed;
> To the unaccustomed eye it seems ugly;
> But the likeness is in that, too, all the same;
> It only needs to be brought out.

It is given to the Dovre-Master (or troll king) in *Peer Gynt* to
sum up in a couple of phrases how he sees these two contrary
philosophies, which he identifies as the human way of life and the
troll way. Among men, he says, the call is 'Man, be thyself!'—or
(to move away from word-for-word literalism) 'To thine own
self be true!' Among trolls, however, this motto is modified (in
Norwegian) by the addition of one small yet 'potent and sunder-
ing' word, which then yields 'Troll, to thyself be—enough!'—or
(again less literally) 'To thine own self be—all-sufficient!' And
here, in these phrases, are defined the poles of the axis about
which the play turns.

Nevertheless the notion, at one time widely canvassed, that
Ibsen created Peer essentially with the intention of amalgamating
in one character all those qualities in the Norwegian temperament
that Brand had so vehemently repudiated, of making a single
compound of the frivolity, the apathy and irresponsibility that
Brand had so fulminated against, should be approached with
caution. Admittedly, an itemized catalogue of Peer's actions—

violent, self-centred, vicious, irresponsible, and indeed on one occasion sheerly murderous—might in sum seem to define a reprehensible villain. Yet, if it really was the drama's original intention to indict Peer, something clearly went wrong; for whilst Brand is admirable though unlovable, Peer is much more a forgivable rogue than he is a despicable villain. No character so given to '*digtning*', to invention, to fabulating, to fantasizing as Peer is could sustain Ibsen's censure for long, one suspects.

Both works are defined on their title-pages as 'dramatic poems', a description not given to any other of Ibsen's works. This in itself reinforces the recognition, which we have confirmed from other first-hand evidence that, uniquely among his 'dramatic' works, they were not originally intended for performance in the theatre, but essentially to be *read*. It becomes clear from a scrutiny of the successive drafts that Ibsen was occasionally uncertain about which metrical form best suited his new purposes. Some of the scenes in the earliest drafts were in fact written in prose; others were first composed in that regular octosyllabic metre, partly iambic, partly trochaic, which had served him for *Brand*. As the work on *Peer Gynt* progressed, however, prose was abandoned; and the more regular metre was to a large extent recast in a looser metrical pattern reminiscent of folk song and ballad poetry. Rhyme, some of it quite audacious and witty, was of course retained, except for the funeral oration in the last act which is in blank verse. The overall result was a swift-moving, idiomatic, often earthy language, which a contemporary reader found very accessible.

Literary scholarship has been assiduous in tracing a whole series of sources—in legend, myth, folk-tale, works of literature, as well as real life—on which Ibsen drew for the composition of *Peer Gynt*. Nevertheless it is clear that by far the most important source for all those multifarious elements that go to make up the work was his own independent creative imagination. From legend, he actually took little more than the name of the chief character: that of a man who still reputedly lived on in peasant memory in Gudbrandsdal, and who Ibsen believed must still have been alive at the beginning of the century or thereabouts. From oral folk tradition, Ibsen was clearly familiar with two passages in Asbjørnsen's standard collection of fairy tales and folk tales: of these, one is an account of the exploits of a boastful hunter called

Per Gynt, including his encounter with the Boyg, with three seter girls, and with divers trolls; and the other was the story of a hunter of a different name who was said to have ridden a runaway wounded reindeer across mountain ridges and glaciers before finally killing it with his knife.

There are also literary antecedents—ranging from Goethe's *Faust* and Oehlenschläger to Wergeland and Hans Andersen— which can be seen (or may be conjectured) as having contributed to the final mix. Individual contemporaries, including friends and acquaintances, public figures and politicians and other writers, frequently provided the raw material for Ibsen's imagination to work on. And finally, and pervasively, there were the memories of his own early life. 'This work contains much that was occasioned by my own childhood,' he was later to confess. 'My mother served, with the necessary exaggerations, as the model for Aase.' And the same store of personal recollection served for the descriptions of life 'in rich Jon Gynt's house'.

But little is gained, particularly for an international audience, by approaching *Peer Gynt* as some kind of *drame à clef*. Most of the allusions—and certainly those even more arcane oblique references—to the 'language debate', to 'Gyntiana', to contemporary chauvinism and its personalities, to wars and political alignments—work effectively and without disruption to what the work is mainly concerned to communicate without any detailed historical framework of reference. Certainly, the more personal of Ibsen's inventions—the Thin Man, the Strange Passenger, the Buttonmoulder, the Dovre-Master, the Woman in Green, together with the absurdist inmates of the Cairo madhouse—are the ones which more lastingly haunt the mind.

The world which Peer Gynt inhabits is one of daunting fluidity, a fairy-tale world of effortless transformations and of disconcerting transpositions; it contrasts sharply with the hard-edge, blueprint world of *Brand* with its severe imperatives, its inflexible compulsions, its frozen and intractable topography. For Peer, the return journey from reality to fantasy and back, from the substance to the shadow and return, requires no frontier formalities. Working and dreaming interpenetrate, fact and fantasy fuse, and all distinctions are blurred. The line between appearance and actuality, between fiction and fact, disappears in one great universe of the imagination. Fears are reborn as only nightmares can shape them; desires are achieved as only dream can fulfil them. The frustrations of one moment become the achievements of the next. If the girls at the village wedding spurn him, the girls on the mountain are ardent and willing. Ostracized and rejected as a suitor by the local community one day, he is welcomed as a potential son-in-law by the troll society the next. Disbelieved and mocked by the village youths when he brags of his exploits, he wins a flattering credulity from the Woman in Green, so that together they can agree that 'black can seem white, and the ugly beautiful; big can seem little, and filth seems clean'. As his mother Aase knows full well, Peer is intoxicated by make-believe as other man are drunk on brandy. His is a world in which wishes *are* horses (or, failing that, pigs!) and beggars *do* ride. Things, he discovers, are no sooner said than they *are* done—like the remotely triggered explosion which sinks the expropriated yacht. For him, distant lands are only a dream away. Fantasy worlds counterfeit the real world; the real one mints again the fantastic. Some creatures, such as the Dovre-Master and the Woman in Green, apparently live a valid life in both; in the case of others, appearances—but only appearances—change, whereby the village wedding guests become recognizable again in the trolls. Sometimes, as with the sound of church bells, reality penetrates fantasy; at other times, as with the Ugly Child, fantasy invades reality. All is an aspect of a single reality/fantasy continuum, wherein fact is a function of fiction, invention of experience, and lies and life are one.

In time, and despite his continuing insistence that the work had not been written for performance, Ibsen began to ponder the possibilities of a theatre production. He fully conceded that the work as it stood was too long, and from the first he accepted the inevitability of major cuts. His first proposed solution to the problem was bizarre: to cut virtually the whole of Act IV and replace it by a kind of tone-poem 'to represent Peer Gynt's wanderings about the world, in which American, English and French melodies might be heard as themes varying and fading...'. He wrote to Edvard Grieg in some detail about how he envisaged 'the necessary music'. Grieg reluctantly accepted the commission, but comprehensively changed the details. At the time he took little pleasure in the work, which he complained had 'a frightfully intractable theme'; and of his piece 'In the Hall of the Mountain King', he confessed: '. . . I literally can't bear to listen to it—so full is it of cow platters, Norwegiomania and self-complacency! But I also expect that people will be able to sense the irony.' History suggests that, alas, the irony was not always so publicly obvious as Grieg hoped it would be. The work was performed for the first time on 24 February 1876 with the Grieg music as we now (almost too well for a balanced understanding of Ibsen's essentially anti-romantic poem) know it.

Its first performance in English translation was at the Garrick Theatre in New York in 1906, with Richard Mansfield in the title-role. In Britain, there was a performance as early as 1908 in Edinburgh at the Queen's Hall; but London had to wait until 1922 for its first performance of substance, with a production at the Old Vic with Russell Thorndike as Peer.

The present version—a translation of sympathetic brilliance by Christopher Fry assisted by Johan Fillinger—was first performed in 1970 at the Chichester Festival, with Roy Dotrice as Peer.

JAMES McFARLANE

SELECT BIBLIOGRAPHY

1. COLLECTED WORKS IN ENGLISH TRANSLATION

There is no lack of editions of Ibsen's plays: these are of greater or
lesser comprehensiveness. William Archer (ed.), *The Collected
Works of Henrik Ibsen*, 12 vols (London, 1906–12), was the first
comprehensive collection in English translation to be published,
and the version by which Ibsen became generally known in the
English-speaking world. James McFarlane (ed.), The Oxford
Ibsen, 8 vols (London, 1960–77), includes the complete plays, together with Ibsen's notes, jottings and earlier draft versions, as
well as critical introductions and other editorial commentary.

2. LETTERS

The Correspondence of Henrik Ibsen, ed. Mary Morison (London,
1905)
Speeches and New Letters, tr. Arne Kildal (London, 1911)
Ibsen: Letters and Speeches, ed. Evert Sprinchorn (New York, 1964;
London, 1965)

3. BIOGRAPHIES

Henrik Jæger, *The Life of Henrik Ibsen*, tr. Clara Bell (London,
1890)
Edmund Gosse, *Ibsen* (London, 1907)
Halvdan Koht, *The Life of Ibsen* (London, 1931; rev. ed. New
York, 1971)
Adolph E. Zucker, *Ibsen the Master Builder* (London, 1929)
Bergliot Ibsen, *The Three Ibsens*, tr. G. Schjelderup (London,
1951)
Michael Meyer, *Henrik Ibsen*, 3 vols (London, 1967–71)
Hans Heiberg, *Ibsen: A Portrait of the Artist*, tr. Joan Tate (London,
1969)

4. CRITICISM (in chronological order)

George Bernard Shaw, *The Quintessence of Ibsenism* (London,
1891; second augmented ed. London, 1913)

George Bernard Shaw, *Our Theatres in the Nineties*. 3 vols
(London, 1932)

James Huneker, *Iconoclasts: a book of dramatists* (London, 1905)

Jeanette Lee, *The Ibsen Secret* (London, 1907)

Haldane Macfall, *Ibsen: the man, his art and his significance* (London,
1907)

Hermann J. Weigand, *The Modern Ibsen: a reconsideration* (New
York, 1925)

Brian W. Downs, *Ibsen: the intellectual background* (Cambridge,
1946)

M. C. Bradbrook, *Ibsen the Norwegian* (London, 1948)

P. F. D. Tennant, *Ibsen's Dramatic Technique* (Cambridge, 1948)

Brian W. Downs, *A Study of Six Plays by Ibsen* (Cambridge, 1950)

Janko Lavrin, *Ibsen: an approach* (London, 1950)

Raymond Williams, *Drama from Ibsen to Eliot* (London, 1952); 2nd
rev. ed. *Drama from Ibsen to Brecht* (London, 1969)

John Northam, *Ibsen's Dramatic Method: a study of the prose dramas*
(London, 1953)

James McFarlane, *Ibsen and the Temper of Norwegian Literature*
(London, 1960, 2nd ed. New York, 1979)

F. L. Lucas, *The Drama of Ibsen and Strindberg* (London, 1962)

M. J. Valency, *The Flower and the Castle* (New York, 1964)

Rolf Fjelde (ed.), *Twentieth-century Views on Ibsen* (New York,
1965)

Daniel Haakonsen (ed.), *Contemporary Approaches to Ibsen*, no. 1
(Oslo, 1966); no. 2 (Oslo, 1971); no. 3 (Oslo, 1977)

James McFarlane (ed.), *Henrik Ibsen*. Penguin critical anthology
(London, 1970)

Orley, J. Holtan, *Mythic Patterns in Ibsen's Last Plays* (Minneapolis, 1970)

Michael Egan (ed.), *Ibsen: the Critical Heritage* (London, 1972)

James Hurt, *Catiline's Dream: an essay on Ibsen's plays* (Illinois,
1972)

Charles R. Lyons, *Henrik Ibsen: the Divided Consciousness* (S. Illinois,
1972)

John Northam, *Ibsen, a Critical Study* (Cambridge, 1973)

Brian Johnston, *The Ibsen Cycle* (Boston, 1975)

Frederick J. and Lise-Lone Marker, *The Scandinavian Theatre: A
Short History* (Totowa, N.J., 1975)

Harold Clurman, *Ibsen* (New York, 1977)

Ronald Gray, *Ibsen—a Dissenting View* (Cambridge, 1977)

Einar Haugen, *Ibsen's Drama* (Minneapolis, 1979)

Edvard Beyer, *Henrik Ibsen* (London, 1979)

J. L. Wisenthal, *Shaw and Ibsen* (Toronto, 1979)

Errol Durbach (ed.), *Ibsen and the Theatre* (London, 1980)

Brian Johnston, *To the Third Empire. Ibsen's Early Drama* (Minneapolis, 1980)

Jane E. Tammany, *Henrik Ibsen's Theatre: Aesthetic and Dramatic Art* (New York, 1980)

Richard Hornby, *Patterns in Ibsen's Middle Plays* (London, 1981)

John S. Chamberlain, *Ibsen: The Open Vision* (London, 1982)

Errol Durbach, *Ibsen the Romantic* (London, 1982)

David Thomas, *Henrik Ibsen* (London, 1982)

Thomas Postlewait (ed.), *William Archer on Ibsen: The Major Essays 1889–1919* (London, 1984)

Daniel Haakonsen (ed.), *Contemporary Approaches to Ibsen*, 5 vols, (Oslo, 1966–84)

John Northam (tr. and ed.), *Ibsen's Poems* (Oslo, 1986)

CHRONOLOGY OF HENRIK IBSEN

1828 20 March Born in Skien, a small timber port about 150 kilometres south-west of Christiania (now Oslo), the second son in a family of six children

1835 June The Ibsen family moves out of town to a smaller house at Venstøp

1843 Leaves Skien for Grimstad to work as an apothecary's apprentice

1846 9 October A servant girl in the household bears him an illegitimate son

1850 12 April His first play, *Catiline*, published, privately and unsuccessfully
   28 April Arrives in Christiania in the hope of studying at the university
   26 September *The Burial Mound* performed at the Christiania Theatre

1851 26 October Takes up an appointment at the theatre in Bergen as producer and 'dramatic author'

1852 Study tour of theatres in Hamburg, Copenhagen and Dresden

1853 2 January *St John's Night* performed at the Bergen theatre

1855 2 January *Lady Inger* performed

1856 2 January *The Feast at Solhoug* performed

1857 2 January *Olaf Liljekrans* performed
   11 August Moves to a post at the Norwegian Theatre in Christiania

1858 25 April *The Vikings at Helgeland* published
   18 June Marries Suzannah Thoresen

1859 His son (and only legitimate child) Sigurd born

1861 Accused of neglect and inefficiency in his post at the Norwegian Theatre

1862 31 December *Love's Comedy* published

1863 October *The Pretenders* published

1864 Leaves Norway and travels via Copenhagen, Lübeck, Berlin and Vienna to Italy, where he remains resident until 1868

1866 15 March *Brand* published. Awarded an annual grant by the Norwegian Parliament

1867 14 November *Peer Gynt* published

1868 October Takes up residence in Dresden

1869 30 September *The League of Youth* published
October–December Travels to Egypt and the Middle East and attends the opening of the Suez Canal, as Norway's representative

1871 3 May His collected *Poems* published

1873 16 October *Emperor and Galilean* published

1874 July–September Summer visit to Norway. Invites Edvard Grieg to compose incidental music for *Peer Gynt*

1875 April Moves from Dresden to Munich for the sake of his son's education

1877 11 October *Pillars of Society* published

1878 Returns to Italy 'for the winter', but remains largely resident there (in Rome) until 1885

1879 4 December *A Doll's House* published

1881 12 December *Ghosts* published

1882 28 November *An Enemy of the People* published

1884 11 November *The Wild Duck* published

1885 June–September Summer visit to Norway
October Takes up residence once again in Munich

1886 23 November *Rosmersholm* published

1887 9 January Berlin performance of *Ghosts* creates a sensation
July–October Summer visit to Denmark and Sweden

1888 28 November *The Lady from the Sea* published

1889 7 June *A Doll's House* performed in London—the first substantial Ibsen production in England

1890 December *Hedda Gabler* published

1891 13 March J. T. Grein's Independent Theatre performs *Ghosts* in London to a storm of criticism

1891 July Leaves Munich for Norway and takes up permanent residence there

1892 11 October His son Sigurd marries Bjørnson's daughter Bergliot
      December *The Master Builder* published

1894 December *Little Eyolf* published

1896 12 December *John Gabriel Borkman* published

1898 Collected editions of his works in Norwegian and German begin publication

1899 19 December *When We Dead Awaken* published

1900 15 March Suffers a stroke, and is unable to do any further literary work

1906 23 May Dies, and is given a public funeral

PEER GYNT

CHARACTERS

AASE,[1] a farmer's widow

PEER GYNT, her son

TWO WOMEN with sacks of corn

ASLAK, a smith

WEDDING GUESTS. STEWARD. FIDDLER, etc.

A MAN and HIS WIFE newly arrived in the district

SOLVEIG and LITTLE HELGA, their daughters

THE FARMER at HAEGSTAD

INGRID, his daughter

THE BRIDEGROOM and HIS PARENTS

THREE HERDGIRLS

WOMAN IN GREEN

DOVRE-MASTER

TROLL COURTIERS. TROLL GIRLS and BOYS. WITCHES. GNOMES,
    GOBLINS and ELVES, etc.

An UGLY CHILD

A VOICE IN THE DARK. BIRD CRIES

KARI, a cottager's wife

MR. COTTON, MONSIEUR BALLON, HERR VON EBERKOPF and HERR
    TRUMPETERSTRAALE, travellers. A THIEF and A FENCE

ANITRA, daughter of a Bedouin sheik

ARABS, SLAVE GIRLS, DANCING GIRLS, etc.

STATUE OF MEMNON (singing), SPHINX OF GIZEH (dumb)

[1] [pron. AW-SË.]

BEGRIFFENFELDT, professor and director of the lunatic asylum in Cairo

HUHU, a language fanatic from the Malabar coast. HUSSEIN, an oriental
   minister. A FELLAH with a mummy

SEVERAL LUNATICS with their WARDERS

NORWEGIAN CAPTAIN and his CREW. A STRANGE PASSENGER

A PRIEST. A FUNERAL PROCESSION. A BAILIFF. A BUTTONMOULDER.
   A THIN MAN

*The action, which begins in the early part of this century and ends close to the
present day [1867], takes place partly in Gudbrandsdal and in the surrounding
mountains, partly on the coast of Morocco, partly in the Sahara Desert, in the
lunatic asylum in Cairo, on the sea, etc.*

ACT ONE

A slope of birch-trees near AASE's *farm. A stream dashes over rocks; an old mill-house on the far side. A hot summer's day.*

PEER GYNT, a sturdy twenty-year-old, comes down the path, followed by AASE, *his mother, a short, slightly built woman, who scolds him angrily.*

AASE. Peer, you're a liar!

PEER [*without stopping*].   No, I'm not!

AASE. Well, swear it's true, then.

PEER.   Why should I swear?

AASE. You see, you daren't! I never heard
 Such a pack of lies.

PEER [*stops*].   The whole thing's true!

AASE [*facing him*]. Would you even try and cheat your mother?
 First you slope off into the mountains
 For weeks when we're busy haymaking
 And go chasing reindeer over the snow;
 Then you come home, a mass of scratches,
 Without your gun or as much as a rabbit;
 And now you stare me in the face
 And think I'll believe this stuff about *hunting*!
 Where did you say you found this buck?

PEER. West, by Gjendin.

AASE [*laughs scornfully*].   Oh, yes, of course!

PEER. I was down-wind of him, frozen stiff;
 I could hear him scraping away the snow
 Behind some trees to get at the moss.

AASE [*as before*]. Of course!

PEER.   I stood, not daring to breathe,
 Heard his crunching hooves, and suddenly

Saw his antlers. Then I wriggled
Along on my belly into a gully
To get a look;—what a buck he was!
So fat and sleek, you couldn't imagine!

AASE. I'm sure I couldn't!

PEER.   Bang! I shot him!
He dropped like thunder on the snow.
The moment he fell I got astride him,
Gripped his left ear, my knife at the ready
To sink in the neck behind the skull;—
Hey! He screamed like a lunatic,
The brute, and in a flash he had scrambled
On to his feet, with a toss of the head
That sent my knife and the sheath flying,
Pinned me round the loins, and locked
His horns against my buttocks: had me
Clamped in a vice; and then we bounded
Off along the Gjendin ridge!

AASE [*involuntarily*]. Jesus help us!

PEER.   Have you seen
That Gjendin ridge? It cuts along
With an edge like a scythe for miles and miles.
You're able to look from that height of snows
And scars and glaciers sheer down
The precipice to the glassy lakes
Sixteen hundred feet below
On either side.—We tore along
The ridge together through the wind.
I've never ridden such a pony!
It seemed as if suns were exploding
Right in my face. Brown-backed eagles
Swam in that vertigo of space
Half-way between us and the lakes,
And dropped away like whirling fluff.
The ice below was crashing and splitting
On shore, but I couldn't hear a sound—
Just the rush of spinning shapes,

A dance of mist that swung and sang
In a frenzy round my ears and eyes!

AASE [*giddy*]. Ah, God help us!

PEER.   Suddenly
When we reached a vicious, break-neck place,
A cock-ptarmigan shot up, scared,
Flapping and cackling, out of the rock
Where he was hiding, almost under
The buck's foot on the ridge. The buck
Shied half-round and jumped sky-high
Out into space with both of us!

[AASE *totters and reaches for a tree-trunk.* PEER GYNT *continues:*]

Behind us, the black wall of mountain,
Below us, the bottomless ravine!
First we bored through layers of fog,
Then sliced across a flock of sea-gulls,
Sent them screaming in all directions.
And down and down and down we went
Until I saw straight underneath me
A gleam, as white as the buck's belly.—
Mother! It was our own reflection
Hurtling up towards the lake's
Glassy surface, as fast as we
Were both careering down to meet it.

AASE [*gasping for breath*]. Peer! God keep me! Be quick, tell me—

PEER. Buck from above, and buck from below,
Collided in a volley of foam.
And there we splashed about for hours
Before we somehow got to shore
On the north side: the buck swimming,
Me hanging on. And I came home.

AASE. And the buck, what happened to the buck, Peer?

PEER. Eh? He's probably still there.

[*Snaps his fingers, turns on his heel, and adds:*]

If you can find him, you can have him.

AASE. And your neck's not broken? No fractured ribs
Or splintered shin? Not a crack to your spine?
O merciful God! What thanks I owe you
For lending my boy such a helping hand!—
You've torn your breeches, but, heaven's above,
That needn't bother us, when I think
What might have happened in a plunge like that!

[*She suddenly stops, with open mouth and eyes, speechless.
Then she turns on him.*]

Ah, it's all a damned rigmarole!
Suffering Christ, you tell such lies!
I remember now this whole concoction;
I heard it all when I was twenty.
It was Gudbrand Glesne it happened to,
Not you, you—

PEER.   Why not me as well?
Things can happen more than once.

AASE [*angry*]. Yes, you can turn a tale inside out,
Polish it up with a lot of swagger,
Disguise it with your fancy feathers
So no one can see the scrawny old carcass.
That's exactly what you've done—
Made it so marvellous and frightful
With twaddle about 'eagle's backs'
And all the rest of the horrible business,
Piling your lies on top of each other
Until in the end I couldn't recognize
A tale I've known the whole of my life.

PEER. If anyone else said that to me
I'd knock him into the middle of next week.

AASE [*weeping*]. Ah, dear God, I wish I was dead:
Sleeping down in the black earth.
Tears and prayers don't touch him at all.—
Peer, you'll be damned, if you aren't already!

PEER. Dear little angel of a mother,
You're right in every word you say.
Come on, be cheerful.

AASE.   Shut your mouth!
  How *can* I, even if I wanted,
  Cursed with a pig of a son like you?
  You never can see how hard it is
  For me, a poor unwanted widow,
  To get nothing out of life but shame.

               [*She cries again.*]

  What's become of the proud days
  Of your grandpa's time, those bags of money
  Old Rasmus Gynt left behind him?
  Your father certainly knew how to spend it;
  Scattered it everywhere like sand,
  Bought up land in every parish,
  Rode about in gilded carriages—
  Where is it now, the fortune he wasted
  On that great winter feast he gave,
  When the guests hurled all the glasses and bottles
  Against the wall—where is it, eh?

PEER. Where are the snows of yesterday?

AASE. Give your mother a chance to speak!
  Look at this farmhouse! Every second
  Window-pane is stuffed with rags.
  Every fence and hedge is down,
  Nowhere for the cows to shelter,
  All the meadows lying fallow,
  And, on top of that, the bailiff
  Coming round here every month—

PEER. For goodness' sake stop whimpering!
  Our luck has often given out
  And sprung up just as high as ever!

AASE. Watered with enough salt tears!
  Oh Lord, what a boy you are,
  The clever-dick you've always been,
  As cocky as you were that day
  The pastor came from Copenhagen,
  Called you by your Christian name
  And swore that even Danish princes

Hadn't as much intelligence.
And your father gave him a horse and sledge
For being so friendly. Ah, dear me,
Life in those days was worth living!
Not a day passed without the captain,
The rural dean and the rest of them
Coming round to eat and drink
Till I thought they'd burst. But when misfortune
Comes you get to know your neighbours.
The house soon emptied and went quiet,
When our Jon-the-money-bag took to the road
With his pedlar's pack.

[*She wipes her eyes on her apron.*]

God knows, you're tall
And strong enough, you should be a help
To your poor old mother. You ought to do
Your duty by the farm, and cherish
What little is left of what we had.

[*She cries again.*]

Heaven help me, little use
You've ever been to me, you lout!
At home you slop about by the fire
Raking the ashes with a poker:
Or else you're round the countryside
Frightening girls away from the parties,
Shaming me whatever you do,
And fighting every oaf you meet.—

PEER [*turning away*]. Let me alone.

AASE [*following him*].   Can you deny
You weren't the cause of all the trouble
In that brawl over at Lunde,
All of you fighting like mad dogs?
Don't say it wasn't you who broke
Blacksmith Aslak's arm, or anyhow
Twisted his finger out of joint?

PEER. Who's been stuffing you with such nonsense?

AASE [*hotly*]. The carter's wife; she heard the yelling!

PEER [*rubbing his elbow*]. So she might. The yells were mine.

AASE. Yours?

PEER.   Yes, mother. *I* got the thrashing.

AASE. What do you mean?

PEER.   He's a hefty chap.

AASE. Who is?

PEER.   Aslak. I ought to know.

AASE. Fiddle-faddle; you make me spit!
    That loafing sot, that good-for-nothing
    Schnaps-gulper—beaten *you*?

                          [*Weeping again.*]

    I've stood years of humiliation
    But for *this* to happen to me
    Is the worst disgrace I ever knew.
    Suppose he is a hefty chap—
    Does it mean you have to be a milksop?

PEER. You moan if I win and moan if I lose.
    [*Laughing.*] You needn't worry—

AASE.   What? Don't say
    You're lying again!

PEER.   I am, for once,
    As a matter of fact; so dry your eyes.

                    [*Clenching his left fist.*]

    I took the blacksmith with these tongs,
    Bent him in half, and used my right
    For a sledge-hammer—

AASE.   You big bully!
    You'll dig my grave, the way you go on!

PEER. I'll give you a better fate than that,
    Twenty thousand times as good.

Kind little walnut of a mother,
You can take my word for it,
One of these days the whole parish
Is going to sing your praises—just
Wait until I accomplish something—
Something absolutely tremendous!

AASE [*with a snort*]. You!

PEER.   Who knows what's round the corner?

AASE. I'd be satisfied if you could manage
To mend the skag in your own breeches!

PEER [*excited*]. I'll be a King—an Emperor!

AASE. O God, just listen!—now he has lost
The final remnant of his wits.

PEER. Oh yes, I will! Just give me time!

AASE. 'Give me time and I'll crow on a dunghill'—
That's what they say, as I remember.

PEER. Well, you wait!

AASE.   You hold your tongue!
You're as stark mad as a man can get.—
And yet we might have made something of you
If you hadn't gone and lost yourself
In a never-ending maze of lies.
Haegstad's daughter had a fancy for you,
You could have had her for the asking
If you had gone about it properly.

PEER. You think so, do you?

AASE.   Yes, I do.
The old man hasn't the strength to argue.
Up to a point he's pig-headed,
But Ingrid gets her way in the end:
She goes ahead, and the old fossil
Tags after, grumbling every step.

                    [*She starts to weep again.*]

Oh, Peer, Peer—all that money—
An heiress! I mustn't think about it.
If only you had put your mind to it
You'd be a splendid bridegroom now—
Instead of a filthy ragamuffin!

PEER [*quickly*]. All right, let's both go courting, then!

AASE. Where?

PEER.   To Haegstad!

AASE.   You poor boy;
Nobody has a chance with her now!

PEER. Why not?

AASE.   Alas, I have to sigh!
Time lost is chances lost.

PEER. Why?

AASE [*sobbing*]. While you were busy riding
Up in the air on a buck's back
She got engaged to Matt Moen!

PEER. What! That jelly-fish? To him?

AASE. Yes, he's the man she's going to marry.

PEER. Wait while I harness the horse and cart.

[*He starts to go.*]

AASE. You needn't trouble. The wedding's tomorrow.

PEER. Who cares? I shall be there tonight.

AASE. Fool! Do you want to shame us worse
By giving them the chance to mock us?

PEER. Don't you fret. It will all be fine!

[*Shouting and laughing.*]

Get a move on! We'll leave the cart;
It would take too long to bridle the nag.

[*He picks her up.*]

AASE. Put me down!

PEER.   Not me, I'll carry you
  All the way to the wedding-feast!

[*He wades into the stream.*]

AASE. Help! God Almighty preserve us!
  Peer! We're drowning—

PEER.   I was born
  For a more glorious end than that.

AASE. Yes—cooling your heels from a gibbet.

[*Pulling his hair.*]

  Oh, you brute!

PEER.   Stop winnicking!
  The bottom is slippery here with slime.

AASE. Mutton-head!

PEER.   That's it, keep swearing;
  That doesn't hurt me!—Ah, you see,
  The ground is shelving up again.

AASE. You dare to drop me!

PEER.   Jiggetty-jig!
  I'll give you a game of Peer and the buck;

[*Curvetting.*]

  I'll be the buck and you can be Peer!

AASE. Oh! I'm going out of my mind!

PEER. There you are, we've got across.

[*He climbs the bank.*]

  Be a good girl, and kiss the buck
  For giving you such a nice ride.

AASE [*boxing his ears*]. There's all the thanks you're going to get!

PEER. Ow! That's a stingy payment!

AASE. Put me down!

PEER.   We're off to Haegstad.
  You're clever: you can argue for me.
  Talk the old curmudgeon round,
  Tell him Matt Moen is a drip—

AASE. Down!

PEER.   And let him know the bargain
  He'll be getting in Peer Gynt.

AASE. Oh yes, you take your oath on that!
  A pretty character I'll give you,
  A lifelike picture, warts and all.
  I'll come straight out with every single
  Devil's trick you ever played—

PEER. You will, will you?

AASE [*kicking with rage*].   I won't draw breath
  Until the old man sets his dog on you
  For the tramp you are!

PEER.   Hm; I'd better
  Go on my own, then.

AASE.   Please yourself,
  I'll follow behind.

PEER.   My dear old mother,
  You haven't the strength.

AASE.   Oh, haven't I?
  I could smash rocks, I'm so angry!
  I could eat flints, I'll tell you that!
  Put me down!

PEER.   Only if you promise—

AASE. Nothing! I'll go to Haegstad with you.
  I'll see they know everything about you!

PEER. If that's the case, you can stay here.

AASE. Never! I'm going to the wedding feast.

PEER. Not on your life.

AASE.   How can you stop me?

PEER. Put you up on the mill-house roof.

[*He puts her there.* AASE *screams.*]

AASE. Take me down!

PEER.   Well, will you listen?

AASE. Rubbish!

PEER.   Please be sensible—

AASE [*throwing a clod of turf at him*].
  Lift me down off this roof this instant!

PEER. If I dared to, of course I would.

[*Coming closer.*]

  Try and remember to sit still.
  Don't stamp, or kick your legs about;
  Or start lugging the stones away—
  Otherwise you won't enjoy it;
  You might fall down.

AASE.   Beast, beast!

PEER. Don't get excited.

AASE.   I only wish
  You'd gone up the chimney like a changeling!

PEER. Tut tut!

AASE.   Twee!

[*She spits.*]

PEER.   You ought to give me
  A mother's blessing on my courtship.
  Do! Will you?

AASE.   I'll give you a thrashing,
  Big as you are!

PEER.   Goodbye, then, mother.
  Have patience. I won't be away too long.

[*He starts to go but turns to lift a warning finger.*]

Remember: don't get over-excited.

[*He goes.*]

AASE: Peer!—God help me, he's really going!
Stag-straddler! Liar! Hey!
Are you listening to me?—No, he's off
Across the fields—! [*She screams.*] Help! I'm giddy!

[TWO OLD WOMEN *with sacks on their backs approach the mill.*]

IST WOMAN. Lord! Who's screaming?

AASE.   Here, it's me!

2ND WOMAN. Aase! Well, you've gone up in the world!

AASE. This much isn't going to help;
Soon, dear God, I'll be in heaven!

IST WOMAN. Pleasant journey!

AASE.   Fetch a ladder;
I must get down! That devil Peer—

2ND WOMAN. Your son?

AASE.   Now you can say you've seen
How he behaves.

IST WOMAN.   With our own eyes!

AASE. Just help me down; I've got to be
Away to Haegstad—

2ND WOMAN.   He's there, is he?

IST WOMAN. You'll get your own back on him all right;
The blacksmith's going to be at the feast.

AASE [*wringing her hands*]. Oh, God look after the wretched boy;
They'll end by killing him!

IST WOMAN.   Often enough
They've talked about it. Comfort yourself
That whatever happens was in the stars.

2ND WOMAN. She's properly gone off her rocker this time!

[*Calling up the hill.*]

Eivind, Anders! Hey, come here!

A MAN'S VOICE. Why, what's wrong?

2ND WOMAN.   Peer Gynt has perched
His mother on the mill-house roof!

SCENE 2   ———————

[*A small hill covered with bushes and heather. The main road runs
behind it; a fence between.*

   PEER GYNT *comes along a footpath, hurries up to the fence and
looks out at the view ahead of him.*]

PEER. There's Haegstad. I shall soon be there.

[*Puts a leg over the fence and hesitates.*]

I wonder if Ingrid will be alone.

[*He shades his eyes, looking down the hill.*]

No. The neighbours are swarming like gnats.
Hm, perhaps I ought to go home again.

[*He draws his leg back again.*]

They snigger at you behind your back,
Their whispering burns into your heart.

[*He goes a few steps away from the fence, and plucks leaves off a
bush.*]

If I had a drink to start me off,
Or if I could walk about invisible,
Or if nobody knew me. A good strong drink's
The way to stop the laughter stinging.

[*He looks round, startled, and hides among the bushes. Some* GUESTS,
with wedding-presents, pass by on their way to the farm.]

A MAN [*conversing*]. His father was a drunk, the mother's
An old crack-pot.

A WOMAN.   No wonder, then,
The boy turned out such a bad lot.

[*They pass by. In a moment* PEER GYNT *comes forward, hot with shame. He stares after them, and mutters:*]

PEER [*softly*]. Was it me they were talking about?

[*With a forced shrug.*] Well, let them!

I don't suppose slander's likely to kill me.

[*He throws himself down on the heather, and lies for some time on his back, his hands behind his neck, staring at the sky.*]

What an odd-shaped cloud! It looks like a horse.
With a man on its back—and a saddle and bridle.
And just behind, an old hag on a broomstick.

[*He laughs quietly to himself.*]

It's mother! She's cussing and carrying-on:
'You beast, you beast! Do you hear what I say, Peer?'

[*His eyes gradually close.*]

Well, she'll be in a fine state now! . . .
Peer Gynt at the head of a great procession,
His horse in a silver cap and gold shoes.
Himself with gauntlet, sabre and scabbard,
And a long cloak with a silk lining.
A glittering company ride behind him
But nobody sits his horse so well
Or sparkles quite like him in the sunlight.
Beside the road there are crowds of people
Lifting their hats and craning to see him.
The women are curtseying. Everyone knows
Emperor Peer Gynt and his thousands of courtiers.
He throws away handfuls of florins and sovereigns
To clink on the road. The whole of the parish
Before very long will be millionaires.
He rides right over the sea, Peer Gynt does;
The King of England waits on the beach.
And, with him, all of England's young women.
When Peer rides up, the English nobles

And the royal family stand to attention.
The King raises his crown, and says—

ASLAK THE SMITH [*to some others as they pass behind the fence*].
There's Peer Gynt, the drunken swine!

PEER [*startled*]. Eh, what, Your Majesty?

ASLAK [*grinning over the fence*].　　　　On your feet
Fellow-my-lad!

PEER.　　　　What the devil—? The blacksmith!
Well, what's on your mind?

ASLAK [*to the others*].　　　　He hasn't got over
That little incident at Lunde!

PEER [*jumping up*]. Are you going, or do I have to make you?

ASLAK. I'm going—but where have you hidden yourself
These last six weeks? Did the fairies get you?

PEER. I've been doing strange things, one way and another.

ASLAK [*winking at the others*]. Go on? Tell us!

PEER.　　　　　　　　It's none of your business.

ASLAK [*after a pause*]. Are you going to Haegstad?

PEER.　　　　　　　　No.

ASLAK.　　　　　　　　At one time
They said it was you that girl was after.

PEER. You black bastard—

ASLAK [*backing away*].　　Keep your shirt on!
If you can't have her, there are plenty of others:
Think, the son of Jon Gynt, what a prize!
Lush widows as well as the girls are there.

PEER. Go to hell!

ASLAK.　　　　I daresay someone would have you.
Good evening! I'll give your regards to the bride.

[*They go off, whispering and laughing.*]

PEER [*looks after them, shrugs, and turns away*].
For all I care the Haegstad girl
Can marry anybody she likes.
No skin off my nose.

[*He looks down at himself.*]

My breeches are torn.
I'm a grim sight. If I'd only got
Something new to put on. [*He stamps his foot.*] If only
I had the knack of a butcher—to chop
The contempt completely out of their innards.

[*Looking suddenly round.*]

What's that? Who sniggered behind my back?
I was sure I heard—No, it was nothing.
I reckon I'll go home to mother.

[*He starts to go up the hill, but pauses again to listen to the sounds from the farm.*]

The dancing has started!

[*He listens, and stares down the hill, gradually descending. His eyes shine and he rubs his hands down his thighs.*]

The place is seething
With girls—seven or eight to a man!
Oh, perishing death,—I've got to be there!—
But how about mother, stuck up on the roof—

[*His eyes stray back to the farm; he jumps up and down, laughing.*]

Hey, look at that! They're dancing the Halling.
Guttorm's a really marvellous fiddler!
It twinkles and leaps like a waterfall.
And all that sparkling flock of girls!—
Yes, perishing death, I've got to be there!

[*He leaps over the fence and is off down the road.*]

_____

SCENE 3

[*The courtyard of Haegstad Farm, the house at the back. Many guests; a lively dance going on on the grass. The* FIDDLER *is sitting on a table. The* STEWARD *stands in a doorway.* SERVANTS *move between the house and out-buildings;* OLDER PEOPLE *sit about talking.*]

A WOMAN [*joining a group sitting on a pile of logs*].
The bride? Yes, of course she's crying a bit.
There's no need to take any notice of that.

STEWARD [*in another group*]. Come on, now, friends, empty the jug.

A MAN. Thanks, but you fill it up too fast.

A BOY [*to the* FIDDLER *as he dances past with a girl*].
Go it, Guttorm, punish those strings!

GIRL. Fiddle away, drown the valley in it!

GIRLS [*in a ring round a dancing* BOY].
Whee, what a leap!

A GIRL.   His legs are like springs!

THE BOY [*dancing*]. The roof's high out here, and the walls are nowhere!

[*The* BRIDEGROOM MATT MOEN *comes whimpering to his* FATHER *who is talking to one or two others, and pulls at his sleeve.*]

BRIDEGROOM. Father, she won't; she's so obstinate.

FATHER. Won't what?

BRIDEGROOM.   She has locked herself in.

FATHER. Well, find the key.

BRIDEGROOM.   I don't know where it is.

FATHER. You're an ass!

[*He turns back to the others. The* BRIDEGROOM *drifts across the yard.*]

A BOY [*from round the house*]. Now there's going to be fun, girls!
Peer Gynt has turned up.

ASLAK [*who has just appeared*]. Who invited him?

STEWARD [*going towards the house*]. Nobody.

ASLAK [*to the girls*].   If he tries to talk to you
Take no notice.

A GIRL [*to the others*]. No, we'll pretend
He doesn't exist.

[PEER GYNT *enters, excited and eager. He stops in front of the girls,
rubbing his hands.*]

PEER.   Who is the gamest
Girl in this bunch?

A GIRL [*as he comes to her*]. I'm not, for one.

ANOTHER [*similarly*]. I'm not, either.

A THIRD.   No, nor me.

PEER [*to a fourth*]. I'll settle for you, till a better turns up.

THE GIRL [*turns away*]. I haven't the time.

PEER [*to a fifth*].   What about you, then?

GIRL [*going*]. I'm just off home.

PEER.   Tonight? Are you mad?

ASLAK [*after a moment, in a low voice*].
You see, she prefers to dance with an old 'un.

PEER [*turning quickly to an* OLDER MAN].
Any spare girls around?

THE MAN.   Find out for yourself.

[*He moves away.* PEER GYNT *is suddenly subdued. He glances shyly
and surreptitiously at the crowd. They stare at him, but no one speaks. He
goes to other groups. Wherever he turns there is silence. When he moves
away they look after him, smiling.*]

PEER [*to himself*]. To be mocked, and whispered about, and grinned at,
It rasps like a sawblade under the file!

[*He slinks along the fence.* SOLVEIG, *holding little* HELGA *by the hand,
comes into the yard with their* PARENTS.]

MAN [*to another standing near* PEER].
Here's that new family.

ANOTHER.   The ones from the west?

IST MAN. Yes, from Hedale.

THE OTHER.   Ah, that's who they are.

PEER [*stepping in front of them, pointing to* SOLVEIG *and addressing the*
    FATHER].
    May I dance with your daughter?

FATHER [*quietly*].   Certainly,
    After we've paid our respects to the family.

                    [*They go in.*]

STEWARD [*offering* PEER *a drink*].
    As you're here you might as well have a drink.

PEER [*staring after them*].
    Thanks, I'm not thirsty. I'm waiting to dance.

    [*The* STEWARD *moves on.* PEER, *smiling, looks towards the house.*]

    Lovely! Who ever saw anything like it?
    She kept looking down at her shoes and her apron!
    She held shyly on to her mother's skirt,
    And carried a prayer-book wrapped in a handkerchief!
    I must look at that girl.

                    [*He goes towards the house.*]

BOY [*coming out with others*]. Have you given up dancing?

PEER. No.

BOY [*takes him by the shoulder to turn him round*].
            Then you're off in the wrong direction.

PEER. Let me get past!

BOY.   Are you scared of the blacksmith?

PEER. Scared?

BOY.   Are you thinking what happened at Lunde?

    [*They go laughing towards the dancers.* SOLVEIG *comes into the doorway.*]

SOLVEIG [*in the doorway*]. Are you the boy who wanted to dance with
    me?

PEER. Yes, yes, yes! Do you have to ask?

[*He takes her hand.*]

Come along!

SOLVEIG.   I mustn't go far, mother said.

PEER. Mother said! Mother said! Were you born last year?

SOLVEIG. Now you're laughing at me!

PEER.   You're such an infant.
Aren't you grown up yet?

SOLVEIG.   I took my first
Communion last spring.

PEER.   Well, what's your name?
It's easier to talk if I know what it is.

SOLVEIG. I'm called Solveig. What are you called?

PEER. Peer Gynt.

SOLVEIG [*withdrawing her hand*]. Oh, goodness!

PEER.   Why, what's wrong?

SOLVEIG. My stocking's untied; I must go and see to it.

[*She leaves him.*]

BRIDEGROOM [*tugging at his mother*].
Mother, she won't!

MOTHER.   Won't? Won't what?

BRIDEGROOM. She won't, mother!

MOTHER.   What?

BRIDEGROOM.   Unlock the door!

FATHER [*angrily under his breath*].
Ah, you're only fit to be tied up
With the calves in a barn!

MOTHER.   Now don't scold him.
Poor lad, he'll do well enough in time.

[*They move away.*]

A BOY [*coming with a crowd of others from the dancing*].
  How about a drink, Peer?

PEER.   No.

A BOY.   Just a drop?

PEER [*looking at him gloomily*].
  Have you any?

BOY.   What do you think?

          [*He pulls a flask out of his pocket and drinks.*]

  Ah!—that singes your stomach!—Want some?

PEER. Let me try it. [*He drinks.*]

2ND BOY.   Now taste some of mine.

PEER. No, thanks.

2ND BOY.   Come on, don't be an idiot;
  Drink up, Peer!

PEER.   Give me a swig, then. [*Drinks again.*]

A GIRL [*quietly*]. Let's be going.

PEER.   Afraid of me, lass?

3RD BOY. Everyone is.

4TH BOY.   You showed us all
  At Lunde what sort of games you get up to.

PEER. I do even better once I get going!

1ST BOY [*whispering*]. Now he's warming up!

SEVERAL [*in a ring round* PEER].   Tell us, do tell us!
  What can you do?

PEER.   I'll show you tomorrow.

BOYS. Show us now!

GIRL.   Honestly, Peer, can you make
  Magic?

PEER.   I can call up the Devil!

A MAN. My grandmother did that before I was born.

PEER. Liar! I do what nobody else can.
 I ordered him once to go into a nut.
 A worm-eaten nut, it was.

SEVERAL [*laughing*].   Oh, yes!

PEER. He cursed and cried, and tried to bribe me
 With this and that—

ONE IN THE CROWD.   But he had to get into it!

PEER. Sure. Then I blocked up the hole with a spigot.
 You should have heard the row he kicked up!

A GIRL. I bet he did!

PEER.   Like a furious bumble-bee.

THE GIRL. Have you still got him inside the nut?

PEER. No, I haven't; he escaped in the end.
 But it's all his fault the blacksmith hates me.

A BOY. Why?

PEER.   Well, I went to the smithy to ask him
 To crack that nut-skull; he said yes, he would.
 He put it on the anvil—but you know Aslak,
 He can't help being heavy-handed,
 Hitting everything with a sledge-hammer—

VOICE. Did he smash the Devil?

PEER.   He came down hard,
 But the Devil was quicker, shot up like a spark
 Right through the ceiling, splitting the wall.

SEVERAL. What about the blacksmith?

PEER.   Left standing there
 With his fingers burnt. We've never been friends
 From that day to this.

[*General laughter.*]

SOMEONE.   That's a good story!

ANOTHER. Just about his best!

PEER.   Do you think I invented it?

A MAN. You didn't need to. I heard most of it
  From my grandfather.

PEER.   Liar! It happened to me.

A MAN. What is there that didn't?

PEER [*throwing up his head*].   I'm able to ride
  Clean through the air on marvellous horses!
  And that's not all I can do, let me say!

  [*A roar of laughter again.*]

VOICE. Take a ride in the air, then!

SEVERAL.   Yes, go on,
  Dear Peer Gynt!

PEER.   You don't have to beg me.
  I'll ride like a hurricane over you lot!
  The whole of the parish will fall at my feet!

OLDER MAN. He's out of his mind!

ANOTHER.   Raving, raving!

A THIRD. Big mouth!

A FOURTH.   Liar!

PEER [*threatening*].   You wait and see!

A MAN [*half drunk*].
  You wait, and your shirt'll be over your head!

OTHERS. Welts on your back, and two black eyes!

  [*The* CROWD *disperses, the older ones angrily, the younger laughing and
  mocking.*]

BRIDEGROOM [*close to* PEER]. Peer, can you really ride through the air?

PEER [*shortly*]. If I want to, Matt; I can do anything.

BRIDEGROOM. Have you got the Invisible Cloak, as well?

PEER. The hat, you mean; yes, of course I've got it.

[*He turns away.* SOLVEIG *crosses the yard, leading* HELGA *by the hand.*]

PEER [*going happily towards them*].
　Solveig! I'm so glad you have come!

[*He grasps her by the wrists.*]

　I'll whirl you round, like the world spinning!

SOLVEIG. Let me go!

PEER. 　　　　　　　Why should I?

SOLVEIG. 　　　　　　　　　　　You're such a wild one.

PEER. So is a reindeer when summer's beginning.
　Come on, girl; don't be so grudging!

SOLVEIG [*withdrawing her arm*].
　I daren't.

PEER. 　　Why not?

SOLVEIG. 　　　　　No, you've been drinking.

[*She moves away with* HELGA.]

PEER. If I'd only stuck my knife through them all!

BRIDEGROOM [*nudging him*].
　Could you help me, do you think, to get at the bride?

PEER [*absently*]. The bride? Where is she?

BRIDEGROOM. 　　　　　　　　　　Locked in the store-room.

PEER. I see.

BRIDEGROOM. So, please, Peer Gynt, will you try?

PEER. No, you'll have to manage without me.

[*A thought strikes him. Softly but sharply.*]

　Ingrid—in the store-room!
　　　　　　　[*Crosses to* SOLVEIG.] Well,
Have you had second thoughts?

[SOLVEIG *tries to leave. He bars her way.*]

                                        I embarrass you
Because you think I look like a tramp.

SOLVEIG [*hastily*]. I don't think that; that isn't true!

PEER. Oh, yes! What's more, I'm slightly drunk;
   I did that on purpose because you offended me.
   Come on!

SOLVEIG.   I daren't now, even if I'd like to.

PEER. Who are you afraid of?

SOLVEIG.   My father, mostly.

PEER. Your father? I get it; he's a devout one,
   Holier-than-thou, eh? Come on, answer!

SOLVEIG. Answer what?

PEER.   Isn't your father
   Pious, and you and your mother as well?
   Tell me the truth.

SOLVEIG.   Let me go in peace.

PEER. No!

                [*Quietly, but still bullying.*]

            I can turn myself into a troll!
At midnight I'll come and stand by your bed.
If you hear something hissing and spitting
Don't comfort yourself it's only a cat.
It will be me! I'll drain your blood
Into a cup, and as for your sister—
I'll gobble her up; I will, because
At night I'm a werewolf; I shall bite
Your loins, and down each side of your spine—

          [*Suddenly changing tone and entreating her.*]

Solveig, do dance with me!

SOLVEIG [*looking at him gravely*]. You were horrible.

[*She goes indoors.*]

BRIDEGROOM [*drifting across the yard*].
   If you'll help, I'll give you a bullock.

PEER.   Come on, then!

   [*They go behind the house. Meanwhile a large crowd, most of them
   drunk, arrive from the dancing. Noise and confusion.* SOLVEIG, HELGA,
   and their PARENTS *come into the doorway with some older people.*]

STEWARD [*to the* BLACKSMITH *who is in the forefront*].
   Calm down, will you?

ASLAK [*taking off his jacket*]. It's the day of reckoning.
   Either me or Gynt must bite the dust.

SOMEONE. Let them have a fight!

OTHERS.   No, keep it to argument.

ASLAK. Fists it has to be; words are punk.

SOLVEIG'S FATHER. Control yourself, man!

HELGA.   Will they beat him, mother?

A BOY. Chivvy him about the lies he tells!

ANOTHER. Kick him off the premises!

A THIRD.   Spit in his eye!

A FOURTH [*to* ASLAK]. Are you backing out?

ASLAK [*throwing down his jacket*].   I'll kill the bleeder!

SOLVEIG'S MOTHER [*to* SOLVEIG].
   Now you see what they think of that foolish boy.

                 [*Enter* AASE, *with a stick in her hand.*]

AASE. Is my son here? He's got a good thrashing
   Coming to him! I'll teach him a lesson!

ASLAK [*rolling up his sleeves*].
   That stick's no good on a body like his!

SOMEBODY. The smith will deal with him!

OTHERS.   He'll flay him!

ASLAK [*spitting on his hands and nodding to* AASE].
   I'll hang, draw, and quarter him!

AASE.   What?
   Hang my Peer? You try and do it;
   He's got a mother with teeth and claws!
   Where is he? [*Calls.*] Peer!

BRIDEGROOM [*running in*].   Oh, it's terrible!
   Father! Mother! Look!

FATHER.   What's happened?

BRIDEGROOM. I can't believe it!—Peer Gynt—

AASE [*shrieking*].   Have they killed him?

BRIDEGROOM. No—Peer Gynt—look up there, on the slopes—

CROWD. He's gone off with the bride!

AASE [*lowering her stick*].   The brute!

ASLAK [*thunderstruck*]. Up the steepest face of the mountain,
   My God!—scrambling like a goat.

BRIDEGROOM [*weeping*]. Carrying her like a pig on his back!

AASE [*shaking her fist towards* PEER].
   Well, I hope you fall—
   [*Screams in terror.*]   Take care what you're doing!

INGRID'S FATHER [*entering bareheaded and white with fury*].
   I'll kill him for this, the ravishing thief!

AASE. God curse me for ever, if I let you!

ACT TWO

A high narrow mountain track. It is early morning, PEER GYNT *hurries sullenly along the path.* INGRID, *still wearing what is left of her wedding finery, tries to hold him back.*

PEER. Get away from me!

INGRID [*crying*].　　　　After this?
　Where can I go?

PEER.　　　　　The further the better.

INGRID [*wringing her hands*]. What lies you've told!

PEER.　　　　　　　　Don't start a row—
　From here we go our different ways.

INGRID. We've sinned, and that binds us together
　For good and all.

PEER.　　　　The Devil take
　All memories, and all women, too—
　Except for one—!

INGRID.　　　What one?

PEER.　　　　　　　　Not you.

INGRID. Who is she, then?

PEER.　　　　　Will you go away?
　Where you came from! Back to your father!

INGRID. Dear heart—!

PEER.　　　　Shut up, will you?

INGRID.　　　　　　　　You can't
　Mean what you say.

PEER.　　　　I can, and do.

INGRID. To tempt me away, and then disown me!

PEER. What have you to offer, tell me that?

INGRID. The Haegstad farm, and more.

PEER.   But have you
  A prayer-book wrapped in a handkerchief?
  Golden hair over your shoulders?
  Do you look shyly down at your dress,
  Your fingers holding your mother's skirt?
  Answer me!

INGRID.   No, but—

PEER.   Did you make
  Your first communion in the spring?

INGRID. No, but, Peer—

PEER.   Are your eyes innocent,
  Can you say No when I ask?

INGRID.   Dear heaven,
  I think he's going out of his mind!

PEER. Does each day I see you become blest?
  Tell me!

INGRID.   No, but—!

PEER [*turning to go*].   What else matters?

INGRID [*intercepting him*].
  You can be hanged if you leave me now;
  Have you realized that?

PEER.   So be it.

INGRID. You can be wealthy and respected
  If you stay with me—

PEER.   I can't afford it.

INGRID [*in tears*]. You persuaded me!

PEER.   You were willing enough!

INGRID. I was desperate!

PEER.   I was hot for a girl.

INGRID [*threatening*].
  Yes, but you're going to pay dearly for it!

PEER. Any price would be cheap to me.

INGRID. Will nothing shake you?

PEER. No.

INGRID. We shall see
  Who wins in the end!

  [*She goes down the hill.* PEER *is silent for a moment, then suddenly
  cries out.*]

PEER. The Devil take
  All memories, and all women, too!

INGRID [*turning and calling back mockingly*].
  Except for one.

PEER. Yes; except for one.

  [*They go their opposite ways.*]

SCENE 2 _____

  [*Near a mountain lake in soggy moorland. A storm is coming up.*
  AASE *enters, calling and searching desperately.* SOLVEIG *has difficulty
  in keeping up with her. Her* FATHER, MOTHER *and* HELGA *follow
  at a little distance.*]

AASE [*tossing her arms and tearing her hair*].
  The world's fury is all against me!
  Heaven, the lakes and the awful mountains!
  Heaven coughs out fog to muddle him!
  Treacherous water is waiting to drown him!
  The mountains mean to slide and bury him!
  And the people are out to kill him, too!
  But, by God, they shan't—I can't do without him!
  The dunce, to let the Devil tempt him!

  [*Turning to* SOLVEIG.]

  Isn't it beyond belief?
  Him, who did nothing but make up tales,

Whose tongue was the only strong thing in him,
Who never did a decent day's work—
I don't know whether to laugh or cry!
But we've stuck together through thick and thin.
Ah yes, I don't mind telling you now,
My husband drank, and spent his time
Fooling and arguing all round the parish,
Throwing away our money like dirt,
While my little Peer and I sat at home.
The best we could do was try and forget it;
I never was good at standing firm.
It's frightful, looking life in the eye;
Better to shrug worry off if you can,
And try not to think too much about it.
So either you take to the bottle, or lies;
That's it: we made do with fairy stories
About princes and trolls and birds and beasts;
And bride-stealing, too. But who would have thought
Those infernal tales would have clung to him so?

[*With renewed anxiety.*]

What was that shriek? A nixie or demon?
Peer! Peer!—On the brow of the hill there!

[*She runs up the rise, looks out over the water as the others join her.*]

Not a thing to be seen!

FATHER [*quietly*].   It's worse for him.

AASE [*crying*]. Oh, my Peer! My poor lost lamb!

FATHER [*nodding gently*]. You're right. He's lost.

ÀASE.   Don't say such things!
He's clever as paint; there's no one like him.

FATHER. You're a foolish woman.

AASE.   Oh, yes, yes,
I'm foolish, but my boy's a marvel.

FATHER [*always softly, his eyes kindly*].
He hardened his heart, and lost his soul.

AASE [*fearfully*]. Oh, no, not that! God isn't so cruel!

FATHER. Does he weep for his burden of sins?

AASE.   Ah, no;
  But he can ride through the air on a buck!

MOTHER. Are you mad?

FATHER.   Do you know what you're saying, woman?

AASE. I say there's no deed too difficult for him.
  He'll show you, if only he lives to do it.

FATHER. You'd do better to see him hang on the gallows.

AASE [*with a scream*]. In Jesus' name!

FATHER.   Perhaps in the hands
  Of the hangman his thoughts would turn to repentance.

AASE [*bewildered*]. Oh, your talk is making my head reel!
  We must find him!

FATHER.   To save his soul.

AASE.   And his body!
  If he's into the bog, we must drag him out.
  If the trolls have got him, we must ring the bells.

FATHER. H'm! Here's a sheep-track—

AASE.   Heaven reward you
  For all your help!

FATHER.   It's a Christian duty.

AASE. Then the rest of them are nothing but heathens!
  Not one among them was willing to come.

FATHER. They knew him too well.

AASE.   He was too good for them.

                    [*She wrings her hands.*]

  Just think, he's in danger of his life!

FATHER. Here's a man's footprint!

AASE.   Then that's the way.

FATHER. At the shepherd's hut we'll divide forces.

[*He walks ahead with his* WIFE.]

SOLVEIG [*to* AASE]. Tell me some more.

AASE [*drying her eyes*].   About my son?

SOLVEIG. Yes, all of it!

AASE [*smiling and lifting her chin*].
                        All? You would soon get tired.

SOLVEIG. You'll get tired of telling it long before
  I'm tired of listening.

SCENE 3

[*Low, treeless knolls just below the high mountain plateau. Tower-
ing peaks in the distance. The shadows are long; it is late in the
day.*

        PEER GYNT *comes leaping into view and halts on the slope.*]

PEER. The whole parish is out in a mob to get me!
  They've armed themselves with sticks and guns,
  With old man Haegstad howling ahead.
  Word's got about Peer Gynt's around somewhere.
  This isn't the same as a scrap with the blacksmith!
  It's life! It gives you the brawn of a bear.

[*He strikes out with his arms and leaps in the air.*]

  You feel you can crush and overthrow,
  Stem the torrent, and root up fir-trees!
  It's life! It makes you iron and air.
  To hell with all those crappy lies!

[THREE HERDGIRLS *run across the hillside, screaming and singing.*]

GIRLS. Trond of Valfjeld! Baard, Aabakken!
  Troll-pack, when the mountains blacken,
  When the sun has taken flight
  Sleep between our arms tonight!

PEER. Who is it you want?

GIRLS.   The trolls! The trolls!

1ST GIRL. Trond do it smoothly!

2ND GIRL.   Baard do it roughly!

3RD GIRL. Our beds are there and no one in them!

1ST GIRL. Roughness is smooth!

2ND GIRL.   Smoothness is rough!

3RD GIRL. With no boys to be had we play with trolls!

PEER. Where are the boys, then?

ALL THREE [*laughing*].   They can't be here!

1ST GIRL. Mine called me sweetheart, his own dear love.
    Now he has married a middle-aged widow.

2ND GIRL. Mine found a girl among the gypsies.
    Now they're tramping the roads together.

3RD GIRL. Mine murdered our bastard baby.
    Now his head grins down from the top of a stake.

ALL THREE. Trond of Valfjeld! Baard, Aabakken!
    Sleep in our arms when the mountains blacken!

PEER [*leaping into their midst*].
    I'm a three-headed troll, and a three-girl man!

GIRLS. Such a fellow, are you?

PEER.   Judge for yourselves!

1ST GIRL. To the hut, to the hut!

2ND GIRL.   There's mead!

PEER.   We'll drink it!

3RD GIRL. Our beds won't be empty this Saturday night!

2ND GIRL [*kissing him*].
    He glows and sizzles like a white-hot poker!

3RD GIRL [*likewise*].
    Like a baby's eyes from a pitch-dark pool.

PEER [*dancing among them*].
  Dread in the heart, but rutting thoughts.
  The eyes laugh, and the throat is choking!

GIRLS [*thumbing noses at the mountains, screaming, singing*].
  Trond of Valfjeld! Baard, Aabakken!
  Troll-pack, when the mountains blacken,
  When the sun has taken flight,
  You're not going to sleep in our arms tonight!

[*They dance away across the hills with* PEER GYNT *in their midst.*]

[*Among the Rondane mountains. Sunset. Shining snow-capped
peaks on every side.* PEER GYNT *enters, wild and distraught.*]

PEER. One castle piled on another!
  The door of that one is dazzling!
  Stay! Will you stay? It's vanishing
  Further and further away!
  The weather-cock up on the vane
  Is lifting its wings to fly;
  Everything goes into shadow,
  The mountain is shut and fastened.
  What are they, the branches and roots
  Growing out of the crack on the hill?
  Giants with herons' feet—
  And now they are vanishing, too.
  Bright wires, like shreds of a rainbow,
  Bore through my eyes to my brain.
  What bells are those, far away?
  And the strange weight on my brow?
  Oh, the pain across my forehead,—
  The grip of a burning crown!
  I can't remember what devil
  Hammered it round my head.

[*He sinks down.*]

  That ride on the Gjendin ridge,
  Invention and damned lies!
  Humping the bride up the steepest

Rock-face—and drunk all day;
Pursued by hawks and kites,
Threatened by trolls and suchlike,
Racketing with crazy wenches;—
Lies and damned invention!

[*He gazes into the sky for a long time.*]

Two brown eagles hovering.
The wild geese flying south.
And here am I, trudging and stumbling
Over my shins in muck.

[*He leaps up.*]

I'll be with you! I'll wash myself clean
In a bath of scouring wind!
I'll go up, and plunge right in
To that bright baptismal font!
Up and over the earth
I'll skim till my mind is serene,
Out and above the sea
Higher than England's king!
You girls can stare, if you like;
My journey's my own concern.
You'll be wasting your time if you wait!
Though I might decide to swoop down.
Where have those eagles got to?
The devil probably took them!
There's the shape of a roof building up,
The eaves, and an angle of wall;
A house growing out of nothing.
You see, the gate's wide open!
Of course, now I recognize it;
It's my grandfather's new farm!
No rags stuffed in the windows;
No fences falling down.
Every window shining;
They're having a feast in the hall.
—I can hear the parson clinking
His knife on the back of his glass;
And the Captain has hurled a bottle

And smashed the mirror to bits.
All right, then, squander the lot!
Quiet, mother, there's more where that came from!
The wealthy Jon Gynt gives a banquet,
Hooray for the family Gynt!
What's all the hubbub about?
Why the shouting and roaring?
They've called for the son of the house:
The parson's proposing my health.
Now—enter Peer Gynt to be valued:
The whole house shakes with his name:
Peer Gynt, born out of greatness,
For what great things you are heading!

[*He rushes forward and collides with a rock. He falls and lies on the ground motionless.*]

SCENE 5   ———————

[*A meadow with tall swaying birchtrees. Stars wink through the leaves, and birds are singing.*

A WOMAN IN GREEN *is walking in the meadow.* PEER GYNT *follows her, making amorous gestures.* THE WOMAN *stops and turns round.*]

WOMAN IN GREEN. Is it true?

PEER [*drawing his finger across his throat*].

As true as my name is Peer;
As true as you're a beautiful woman!
Will you have me? You'll see how well I turn out;
You needn't weave, you needn't spin,
You can eat so much you'll give at the seams.
What's more, I won't drag you about by the hair.

WOMAN IN GREEN. Nor beat me, either?

PEER.   Now is that likely?
Kings' sons don't go around beating women.

WOMAN IN GREEN. Are you a king's son?

PEER.   Yes, I am.

WOMAN IN GREEN. And I am the King of the Dovres' daughter.

PEER. Really? Well, there's a happy coincidence.

WOMAN IN GREEN. His palace is deep in the Ronde mountain.

PEER. My mother's is grander, I should say.

WOMAN IN GREEN. Do you know my father? King Brosse, his name is.

PEER. Do you know my mother? Her name's Queen Aase.

WOMAN IN GREEN. When father's angry, the mountains crack open.

PEER. They belch if my mother so much as grumbles.

WOMAN IN GREEN. My father can kick to the top of the roof-tree.

PEER. My mother can ride through a river in flood.

WOMAN IN GREEN. Are those rags the only clothes you've got?

PEER. Ah, you should see my Sunday outfit!

WOMAN IN GREEN. I wear silk and gold every day of the week.

PEER. It looks to me like shoddy and straw.

WOMAN IN GREEN. Yes, but you've got to bear in mind
In my country everything we own
Has two different ways of being looked at.
If ever you visit my father's house
At first you might believe you stood
In a wilderness of scattered stones.

PEER. Extraordinary; it's the same with us.
You'll think our gold is dirt and trash;
You may even imagine the sparkling windows
Are stuffed up with old stockings and rags.

WOMAN IN GREEN. Black can be white, and the ugly beautiful.

PEER. Big can seem little, and filth seem clean.

WOMAN IN GREEN [*throwing her arms round his neck*].
Oh, Peer, I can see we were made for each other.

PEER. Like a leg and breeches, like faggots and peas.

WOMAN IN GREEN [*calling across the meadow*].
Wedding-day horse! Wedding-day horse!
Come at the call, my wedding-day horse!

[*A gigantic pig comes running in, with a rope's end for a bridle, an old sack for a saddle.* PEER GYNT *vaults on to its back and lifts the* WOMAN *up in front of him.*]

PEER. Yoicks! We'll streak through the gates of Ronde!
  Gee-up, gee-up, my galloping grey!

WOMAN IN GREEN [*lovingly*].
  And I've been so dull and moody lately—
  You never know what will happen to you!

PEER [*whipping the pig as they trot off*].
  You can tell who's well-born by the bloodstock they ride!

SCENE 6 _____

[*The Throne Room of the Dovre-Master. A great crowd of* TROLL
COURTIERS, GNOMES *and* GOBLINS. *The* DOVRE-MASTER *on the
throne, crowned, and holding a sceptre. His* CHILDREN *and*
RELATIVES *on either side of him.* PEER GYNT *stands before him.
Much commotion.*]

TROLLS. Kill him! The son of a Christian has raped
  The heart of the Dovre-Master's daughter!

TROLL CHILD. Can I cut one of his fingers off?

2ND CHILD. Can I pull his hair?

TROLL GIRL.   Let me bite his crutch!

WITCH [*with a ladle*]. Render him down to make a soup!

2ND WITCH [*with a chopper*].
  A roast on a spit, or stew in a pot!

DOVRE-MASTER. Cool down!
                    [*Beckoning his* COUNSELLORS:]
                  We don't want to have any bragging.
  We've been losing ground these last few years;
  It's a question whether we'll stand or fall,
  Human help could be very useful.
  Besides, he's almost without a blemish,
  And well-built, too, by the look of him.

It's true he has only got one head,
But, then, my daughter's no better off.
Three-headed trolls have gone out of fashion;
Even two-headed ones aren't seen very often,
And the heads of those are pretty inferior.

[*To* PEER GYNT.]

So you want my daughter?

PEER.   I do: and also
Your kingdom as dowry.

DOVRE-MASTER.   You shall be given
Half when you marry, the rest when I'm dead.

PEER. That's fair enough.

DOVRE-MASTER.   Yes, but not so fast;
We haven't settled your part of the bargain.
Promises have to be made on your side.
If you break even one the contract's void.
You'll never get out of here alive.
First, you must banish from your mind
Everything outside this kingdom;
Day must be shunned, and all its deeds,
And any place where the light gets in.

PEER. With a throne in prospect, that's no great drawback.

DOVRE-MASTER. Next—I must find out how clever you are.

[*He rises from his seat.*]

OLDEST COURTIER [*to* PEER GYNT].
Let's see how your wisdom-teeth can crack
The nutty problems he's going to propound.

DOVRE-MASTER. What's the difference between a troll and a human?

PEER. No difference at all, it seems to me.
Big trolls roast you, small trolls scratch you;
It's the same with us, when we're brave enough.

DOVRE-MASTER. You're right; we're alike in that and much else.
But morning is morning, and evening is evening,

So there is a difference, after all.
Allow me to tell you what it consists of:
Out there, under the radiant sky,
They say 'To thine own self be true.'
But here, in the world of trolls, we say
'To thine own self be—all-sufficient!'

TROLL COURTIER [*to* PEER GYNT].
Do you grasp his meaning?

PEER.   It seems—obscure.

DOVRE-MASTER. 'Sufficient', my son, that potent, thundering
Word you must bear on your coat-of-arms.

PEER [*scratching his head*].
Yes, but—

DOVRE-MASTER. *Must*, if you're going to rule here!

PEER. Yes, well, all right; it might be worse.

DOVRE-MASTER. And then you must learn to appreciate
Our simple, homely way of living.

[*He beckons; two* TROLLS *with pigs' heads, white nightcaps, etc.,
bring food and drink.*]

From the cow we get cake, from the bullock mead;
Don't ask if the taste is sweet or sour;
The main thing is, and don't you forget it,
It's all home-made.

PEER [*pushing it away*]. Home-made the devil!
I'll never get used to this country's habits.

DOVRE-MASTER. The bowl goes with it, it's made of gold.
Who has the bowl has my daughter, too.

PEER [*pondering*]. Well, it's said 'You must master your instincts';
I suppose in time it won't seem so sour.
Here goes!

[*He obeys.*]

DOVRE-MASTER. Very sensible. You spit?

PEER. I hope to get used to it after a while.

DOVRE-MASTER. You must now get out of your Christian clothes;
In Dovre we pride ourselves that nothing
Comes from the valley, all mountain-made,
Except the silk bow on the tip of the tail.

PEER [*indignant*]. I don't have a tail!

DOVRE-MASTER.   We'll get you one.
Steward, fetch my Sunday tail for him.

PEER. No fear! Are you trying to make a fool of me?

DOVRE-MASTER. You can't woo my daughter with a bare backside.

PEER. Turning men into beasts!

DOVRE-MASTER.   Not at all, my son;
I'm making you an acceptable suitor.
You will have a patriotic yellow
Bow to wave, to your lasting honour.

PEER [*thoughtfully*]. They say that a man is only dust.
One should make some concession to custom and fashion.
Tie away!

DOVRE-MASTER. You're a pleasant amenable fellow.

COURTIER. Now show us how well you can flourish and wag it!

PEER [*annoyed*]. Anything else you want me to do?
Do you ask me to give up my Christian faith?

DOVRE-MASTER. You're welcome to keep that undisturbed.
Belief is free; we don't tax that.
What makes a troll is the outward style.
So long as you match us in manner and dress
You can believe what horrifies *us*.

PEER. In spite of the many provisos, you seem
More reasonable than I thought you were.

DOVRE-MASTER. We trolls aren't as bad as we are made out.
That's one more distinction between you and us.—
Well, so much for the serious business.
Now we can gladden our ears and eyes.

Musicians, ripple the Dovrean harp!
Dancers, tap the Dovrean floor!

[*Music and a dance.*]

COURTIER. How do you like it?

PEER.   Like it? Well—

DOVRE-MASTER. Don't be afraid to speak your mind.
What do you see?

PEER.   A hideosity.
A cow twangs a gutstring with its cloven hoof.
A sow in tights jigs to the strumming.

COURTIERS. Eat him!

DOVRE-MASTER.   Remember, his senses are human!

TROLL MAIDENS. Tear off his ears, rip out his eyes!

WOMAN IN GREEN [*weeping*]. To have to endure such things being said
When my sister and I are playing and dancing!

PEER. Oh, it was you? You mustn't take
A joke at a party for anything serious.

WOMAN IN GREEN. Do you *mean* that?

PEER.   I swear the dancing and music
Were both—quite good, or the cat can have me.

DOVRE-MASTER. A curious thing, this human nature.
It takes such a lot of getting rid of.
If it gets a gash from struggling with us
It may bear a scar, but the wound soon heals.
My son-in-law here is as docile as any:
Willing to take his Christian clothes off,
Willing to drink the home-made mead,
Willing to have a tail tied on him,—
So willing, in fact, to do all we ask him
I took it for granted the old Adam
Had been shown the door once and for all.
But you see he's back in the saddle again.
Well, well, my son, you have to be cured
Of this tyrannical human nature.

PEER. What will you do?

DOVRE-MASTER.   I'll scratch the left eye
A little, to help you see obliquely;
But all that you see will be rich and strange.
Then I'll take the right one out completely—

PEER. Are you drunk?

DOVRE-MASTER [*placing some sharp instruments on the table*].
                        Here are the glazier's tools.
You must go in blinkers, like a dangerous bull.
Then you'll know how to value the charms of your bride—
And your eyes will never deceive you again
With dancing pigs and musical cows.

PEER. This is raving!

OLDEST COURTIER.   The thoughts of the Dovre-Master.
He has wisdom; it is you who are mad.

DOVRE-MASTER. Consider how much harm and anxiety
You will save yourself for the rest of your life.
Your eyes are the well-spring, don't forget,
Of tears, and their burning, bitter flow.

PEER. True enough; and the Bible says:
If thine eye offend thee, pluck it out.
But listen! When will the eyesight heal
And be human again?

DOVRE-MASTER.   Never, my friend.

PEER. Never? For ever, then, thanks very much.

DOVRE-MASTER. Where are you off to?

PEER.   I'll find my way.

DOVRE-MASTER. No, stop! The way in is easy enough,
But the gates aren't made to open outwards.

PEER. Do you think you're going to force me to stay here?

DOVRE-MASTER. Come, use your intelligence, Prince Peer!
You've a natural gift for being a troll.

Isn't he almost a troll already?
And surely that's what you want?

PEER.   God knows
I do. For a bride, and a well-run kingdom
Into the bargain, I realize
Something has got to be given up.
But there's a limit to everything.
I've accepted the tail, that's right enough;
But I guess I can slough what the steward tied on;
I've got out of my breeches, hardly worth wearing;
But it's easy enough to pull them on
And do up the buttons; and I dare say
I can also unburden myself
Of the habits you have here. I'm perfectly happy
To swear a cow is really a girl,
Later on I can always eat my words;—
But to know you can't ever free yourself,
Or die a respectable human death,
To be stuck as a troll for the rest of your days,
This thing of having no line of retreat,
As the text-book says, which you so insist on,
That's a condition I'll never give in to.

DOVRE-MASTER. Now, by corruption, I shall lose my temper.
You'll find I'm not someone to trifle with.
You sun-bleached ninny! Do you know who I am?
First you come and solicit my daughter—

PEER. A damnable lie!

DOVRE-MASTER.   You have to marry her.

PEER. Do you accuse me of—

DOVRE-MASTER.   What? You can't
Deny that you lusted after her?

PEER [*with a snort*]. If I did? Who cares a fig about that?

DOVRE-MASTER. You human beings are all alike.
Lip-service to your souls, but you worship
Only what you can grab with your fists.
So you really think lust doesn't matter?

Wait! You will soon have proof that it does—

PEER. You won't hook me with a bait of lies!

WOMAN IN GREEN. Peer, before the year's at an end,
You'll be a father.

PEER.   Open the doors!
Let me get out.

DOVRE-MASTER.   Your cub will come after you
Wrapped in a buckskin.

PEER [*wiping his brow*].   Oh, let me wake!

DOVRE-MASTER. We should send him, no doubt, to your royal castle?

PEER. Who cares? You can put him on the parish!

DOVRE-MASTER. Very well, Prince Peer; it's just as you like.
But one thing's certain, what's done is done,
Which means your offspring is bound to grow.
Mongrels mature at a fearful rate.

PEER. Look, sir, you don't have to be so stubborn.
Woman, be reasonable. Come to terms.
As it happens I'm neither a prince nor rich;
Whether you weigh me or measure me
You'll find I'm simply not worth keeping.

[*The* WOMAN IN GREEN *faints and is carried out by* TROLL MAIDENS.]

DOVRE-MASTER [*looking at him contemptuously before speaking*].
Dash him to pulp against the rocks!

YOUNG TROLLS. Oh, father, can we play owls-and-eagles?
The wolf-game! Grey mouse and green-eyed cat!

DOVRE-MASTER. Be quick, then. I'm vexed and sleepy. Goodnight.

[*He goes.*]

PEER [*chased by the* YOUNG TROLLS].
Let me alone, you rags of hell!

[*Tries to get up the chimney.*]

YOUNG TROLLS. Hobs and goblins! Bite his buttocks!

PEER [*trying to get through the trap-door to the cellar*].
  Ow!

YOUNG TROLLS. Close the hatches!

COURTIER.   What happiness
  For the youngsters!

PEER [*struggling with a* TROLL CHILD *who is biting his ear*].
  Will you get off me, you horror!

COURTIER [*rapping* PEER *over the knuckles*].
  Ruffian, that's no way to treat a princeling!

PEER. A rat-hole! [*He runs to it.*]

YOUNG TROLL.   Brother gnomes, block it up!

PEER. The old one was bad, but the kids are worse!

YOUNG TROLL. Flay him!

PEER. If only I were the size of a mouse!

                                    [*He runs around.*]

YOUNG TROLLS [*closing in on him*].
  Fence him round! Fence him round!

PEER [*weeping*]. Oh, to be a bed-bug! [*He falls.*]

YOUNG TROLLS.   Now for his eyes!

PEER [*buried under the* TROLLS].
  Help, mother, I'm dying!

                    [*Church bells ring in the distance.*]

YOUNG TROLLS. Bells in the mountains! The holy-man's cows!

  [*The* TROLLS *fly shrieking in disorder. The Throne Room collapses;
  everything disappears.*]

SCENE 7 _____

  [*Pitch darkness.* PEER GYNT *is heard slashing and flailing about
  with a great bough.*]

PEER. Give an answer! Who are you?

VOICE [*in the dark*].   Myself.

PEER. Get out of my way!

VOICE.   Go round and about.
   This heath is big enough.

   [PEER GYNT *tries to get through at another place, but hits against
   something.*]

PEER.   Who are *you*?

VOICE. Myself. Are you able to say the same?

PEER. I can say what I like; and my sword can smite!
   Whee! Look out for the stroke! Saul slew
   His thousands, Gynt his tens of thousands!

                  [*Slashing about him.*]

   Who *are* you?

VOICE.   Myself.

PEER.   I've had enough
   Of that damnfool answer. It doesn't clear up
   Anything. *What* are you, then?

VOICE. The great Boyg.

PEER.   Oh, are you, indeed?
   At least what was black is becoming grey.
   Out of the way, Boyg!

VOICE.   Go round and about!

PEER Straight on! [*Hacking and slashing.*]

                  I felled him!

   [*He tries to advance, but meets opposition.*]

                          Is there more than one of you?

VOICE. The Boyg, Peer Gynt! The only one.
   The Boyg that's unharmed, and the Boyg that is wounded.
   The Boyg that is dead, and the Boyg that's alive.

PEER [*throwing away the branch*].
   Trolls blunted my sword, but I've got my fists!

                  [*Pummels his way forward.*]

VOICE. Yes, trust to your fists; trust to your body.
  Well done, Peer Gynt, you'll get to the top.

PEER [*retreating*]. Forward or back, it's the same distance;
  Out or in, it's equally narrow!
  He's here! and there! And round the corner!
  When I seem to get clear I'm surrounded again.—
  Let me see you! What kind of thing are you?

VOICE.   The Boyg.

PEER [*groping*]. Neither dead nor alive. A slime, a mist.
  Not even a shape! It's worse than fighting
  A horde of growling, sleep-sodden bears!
  [*Screaming.*] Hit back, can't you?

VOICE.   The Boyg isn't mad.

PEER. Hit me!

VOICE.   The Boyg hits at nothing.

PEER.   Give battle!
  I'll make you!

VOICE.   The great Boyg wins without battle.

PEER. If there was only a pinching goblin,
  Or even a year-old baby troll!
  Just something to fight with. But here there's nothing.
  He's begun to snore! Boyg!

VOICE.   What is it?

PEER. Use force!

VOICE.   The great Boyg conquers
  Everything without an effort.

PEER [*biting his own arms and hands*].
  Teeth and nails into the flesh!
  I have to feel the flow of my blood.

            [*A sound like the wing-beat of great birds.*]

BIRD-CRIES. Is he coming towards us, Boyg?

VOICE [*in the dark*]. Yes, inch by inch.

BIRD-CRIES. Sister birds
  Flying far off, meet with us here!

PEER. Solveig, if you mean to save me
  Do it quickly! Don't stand staring
  Down at the ground. Hurl your prayer-book
  With the silver clasp straight at his head!

BIRD-CRIES. He's flagging!

VOICE. We have got him.

BIRD-CRIES. Sisters! Hurry!

PEER. It's too high a price to pay for life,
  To bear any more of this fearful game.

[*He sinks down.*]

BIRD-CRIES. Boyg, he's down! Take him! Take him!

[*Church bells and hymn-singing are heard in the distance.*]

VOICE [*shrinking away to nothingness with a gasp*].
  He's too strong. There are women behind him.

SCENE 8

[*Sunrise. The hillside outside AASE's mountain hut. The door is
shut; everything deserted and silent. PEER GYNT is asleep by the wall.
He wakes up, looks round with heavy eyes. He spits.*]

PEER. I'd give anything for a pickled herring!

[*He spits again, and catches sight of HELGA who enters with a basket
of food.*]

  Hey, chick, it's you! What are you here for?

HELGA. Because Solveig—

PEER [*jumping up*]. Where is she?

HELGA. Behind the hut.

SOLVEIG [*hidden*]. If you come any nearer I'll run away.

PEER [*stopping*]. Afraid that I shall put my arms round you,
  Is that the trouble?

SOLVEIG   Shame on you!

PEER.   Guess
  Where I was last night! The Dovre-Master's
  Daughter is plaguing me like a horse-fly.

SOLVEIG. It was lucky, then, that we rang the bells.

PEER. Peer Gynt's not the boy to be seduced.
  What do you say?

HELGA [*weeping*].   Oh, she's going! Wait for me!

                  [*She runs after* SOLVEIG.]

PEER [*catching her by the arm*].
  Look what I've got in my pocket for you!
  A silver button! You can have it to keep,
  But put in a good word for me, will you?

HELGA. Let go; don't hold me!

PEER.   Here it is.

HELGA. Let me go! The food's over there.

PEER. If you don't, God help you—

HELGA.   I'm frightened of you!

PEER [*meekly releasing her*].
  All I meant was, ask her not to forget me!

                  [HELGA *runs off.*]

ACT THREE

In the depth of the pine forest. A grey autumn day. Snow is falling.
PEER GYNT, *in his shirt sleeves, felling timber for building.*

PEER [*hewing a big fir-tree with twisted branches*].
Ah, yes, you are strong, you mindless giant,
But that won't help, you've got to come down.

[*Chopping again.*]

I notice you're wearing your chain-mail,
But I'll hack through that, hard as it is.
Yes, you can shake your sinewy arm;
You're right to feel indignant and furious;
Even so, I must bring you to your knees!

[*He breaks off his work.*]

Lies! It's only an old tree.
Lies! It isn't a giant in armour;
It's a fir-tree with a craggy bark.
Cutting down trees is hard work,
And hell if you're dreaming while you do it.
It will have to stop—this wool-gathering
And floating away in broad daylight.—
You're outlawed, my boy, condemned to the forest.

[*He chops energetically for a bit.*]

Yes, you're an outlaw. You haven't a mother
To bring you food and lay the table.
If you're hungry you must help yourself,
Get it raw from the forest and river,
Split your logs and make your fire,
Busy about, set things to rights.
If you want clothes, you must kill a deer,
If you want a house, you must quarry the stone,
Cut the planks for the timber in it
And carry them to the building site.

[*He lowers his axe and stares in front of him.*]

It will be splendid. A tower and weather-cock
Soaring up above the roof.
And then I'll carve on the end of the gable
A mermaid, fish from the navel downwards.
Latches and weather-cock made of brass;
And I'll have to find some glass somewhere.
Passers-by will ask what it is
Shining out across the hillside.

[*He laughs contemptuously.*]

Bloody lies! There you go again.
You're an outlaw, idiot! [*Chopping fiercely.*]
                    All you need
To keep out the weather is a log cabin.

[*He looks up at the tree.*]

He's starting to rock. Only a kick!
There he goes, crashing down;—
The undergrowth sighing and shuddering!

[*He begins to lop off the low branches. Suddenly, with uplifted axe, he stops to listen.*]

There's someone after me!—That's your game,
Old man Haegstad—to creep up behind me.

[*He hides behind a tree and peeps out cautiously.*]

A boy! By himself. He's looking scared,
And keeping his eyes skinned. What's he hiding
Under his jacket? A sickle. He looks
Round, and puts a hand flat on the fence.
What's he up to? He seems to be bracing himself to—
Ach! He has cut his finger off!
The whole finger off! And bleeds like an ox.—
Now he has bound it up, and run off.

[*He gets to his feet.*]

What spunk! An irreplaceable finger!
Right off! And no one making him do it.

Ah, now I remember! It's the only way
To avoid being called up for the army.
That's it. They were going to send him to war;
And the boy, not surprisingly, objected.—
But to hack it off—part with it for ever?—
To consider it, yes; wish it; even
Prepare yourself for it; but to *do* it!
No; that's something I can't understand.

[*He shakes his head and goes on with his work.*]

SCENE 2

[*A room in* AASE's *house. Everything is in disorder. Chests standing open, and clothes scattered about. A cat is on the bed.*
AASE *and* KARI, *the cottager's wife, are packing and clearing up.*]

AASE [*crossing the room*].
  Kari, listen—

KARI.   What is it, love?

AASE [*crossing back*].
  Do you know—where is—what has become of—
  You can tell me—where *is* that—what am I looking for?
  I'm so befuddled. Where's the key to that chest?

KARI. In the keyhole.

AASE.   What's that clattering noise?

KARI. It's the last load on its way to Haegstad.

AASE [*weeping*]. I'd be glad if the load was me in my coffin!
  Ah, what we mortals have to suffer!
  God pity me! The whole house stripped bare!
  What old Haegstad left the bailiffs went off with.
  They haven't left me the clothes I stand up in.
  They should be ashamed of that cruel sentence!

[*She sits on the edge of the bed.*]

The farm and the land gone out of the family.
Old Haegstad was bad enough, but the law

Was worse; no help, and no sympathy,
And Peer gone away; no one to advise me.

KARI. You can sit tight here, in this house, till you die.

AASE. Yes, the cat and I, living on charity.

KARI. Poor soul, your boy has cost you dearly.

AASE. Peer? You're as soft-headed as I am!
Didn't Ingrid get safely home in the end?
They should have laid the blame on the Devil;
He was the sinner and no one else;
He tempted my boy, the ugly monster!

KARI. Hadn't we better send for the priest?
Maybe you're not as well as you think.

AASE. For the priest? Yes, perhaps we should.

[She starts up.]

No, my God, I can't! I'm the boy's mother;
I must help him; that's no more than my duty;
I must do my best, when the rest let him down.
They've left him this coat. I'd better mend it.
For two pins, I'd hang on to this fur-rug, too.
Where are the stockings?

KARI.   Over there
With the rest of the rubbish.

AASE *[rummaging around]*.   What's this? Bless me,
It's the old casting-ladle, Kari!
He used to play being buttonmoulder
With this, melt and mould and stamp them.
He came in one day when we had company
And asked his father for a lump of tin.
Not tin, Jon said, but here's a real coin,
Silver, to show you're Jon Gynt's son.
God forgive him; but he was drunk,
And, tin or gold, it was all the same to him.
Here are the stockings. Nothing but holes;
They'll take some darning.

KARI.   They certainly will.

AASE. When I've done that I'll go to bed;
I feel so poorly, and weak and shivery.

[*Joyfully.*]

Two wool shirts, Kari! They left them behind!

KARI. Yes, so they did.

AASE.   What a bit of luck!
You'd better put one of them aside.
No, wait, I think we should have them both;
The one he's wearing is almost threadbare.

KARI. That would be sinful, mother Aase!

AASE. May be; but the priest will absolve us of it,
Along with all the rest of our sins.

SCENE 3   ————————

[*Outside a newly-built hut in the forest. Reindeer antlers over the
door. Deep snow lying. It is dusk.*
    PEER GYNT *is outside the door, fastening a large wooden bolt.*]

PEER [*with occasional chuckles*].
You must have a lock; a lock to secure
The door against trolls, and men and women.
You must have a lock; a lock to shut out
All the pestering hobgoblins.—
They come rattling and knocking after dark:
Open up, Peer Gynt, we're as cunning as thoughts!
We fuss under the bed, rake about in the ashes,
And flail in the chimney like fiery dragons.
Aha! Peer Gynt; how can planks and nails
Keep out the pestering goblin thoughts?

[SOLVEIG *enters on skis across the clearing. She has a shawl over her
head and carries a bundle.*]

SOLVEIG. God speed your work. Don't send me away.
You brought me here, and must welcome me.

PEER. Solveig. It can't be—! Yet it is!
   And you're not afraid to come so close.

SOLVEIG. One message you sent by little Helga;
   Others came with the wind and silence.
   More came with all your mother told me.
   They grew and multiplied in my dreams.
   The heavy nights and empty days
   Insisted that I should come to find you.
   Down there life seemed to have come to an end;
   I hadn't the heart to laugh or cry.
   I couldn't be sure what you were thinking,
   I was only sure what I had to do.

PEER. But your father?

SOLVEIG.   In all God's universe
   I have no one now to call father or mother.
   I have left them.

PEER.   Solveig, my beautiful—
   To come to me?

SOLVEIG.   Yes, you alone;
   There's no one else to befriend and comfort me.

            [In tears.]

   Leaving my sister was the worst;
   Or still worse, parting from my father;
   Or worst of all, from my dearest mother;—
   No, God forgive me, the hardest grief
   Was leaving all of them—all of them!

PEER. And you know the sentence I got in the spring?
   Farm, land, and inheritance confiscated.

SOLVEIG. It wasn't because of what you owned
   That I came away from those I loved.

PEER. And you know the rest? They're free to kill me
   Whenever they see me outside the woods.

SOLVEIG. Coming over the snow I asked my way.
   When they wanted to know where I was going
   I told them, 'Home'.

PEER.   Then away with hammer,
  And nails and planks! I'm not going to need
  Protecting now against goblin thoughts.
  If you're ready to share an outlaw's life
  A blessing will hover over this hut.
  Solveig! Let me look at you!
  Don't come too near! To look at you!
  You are like light and the pure air.
  Let me lift you! Like thistledown.
  When I carry you I shall never be tired.
  I won't muss you. With arms outstretched
  I'll hold you out there, my lovely warm one!
  How could I guess I could bring you to me?
  But I have longed for it night and day.
  You can see how I've been hewing and building;
  It will have to come down; too bare to house you.

SOLVEIG. Bare or not, it's what I like.
  It's so easy to breathe up here in the wind.
  Down there it was stifling; it seemed to crush me;
  That was partly what scared me into leaving.
  But now I can hear the fir-trees soughing,
  Great silence and singing! This is my home.

PEER. Are you certain of that? For the rest of your days?

SOLVEIG. The road I have taken doesn't lead back.

PEER. You're really mine! Come into the house!
  Let me see you indoors. Go in! I'll fetch
  Some wood for the fire, to light and warm you!
  Then rest happy, and never be cold.

  [*He opens the door.* SOLVEIG *goes in. He stands still for a moment. Then he laughs for joy and leaps in the air.*]

  My king's-daughter! Found and won!
  Now I shall build a palace on rock!

  [*He picks up his axe and starts to go. An* ELDERLY WOMAN *in a green-tattered dress steps out of the woods. An* UGLY CHILD, *carrying a jug of ale, limps after her, holding her skirt.*]

WOMAN. Good evening, slippery friend.

PEER.   Who are *you*?

WOMAN. An old acquaintance. I live near by.
  We're neighbours.

PEER.   Indeed? I don't know about that.

WOMAN. While you built your hut mine grew beside it.

PEER [*going*]. I'm in a hurry—

WOMAN.   As you always were;
  But I trudge behind, and I'll catch you at last.

PEER. You've made some mistake—

WOMAN.   I made a mistake
  Once, in the past, when you promised so much.

PEER. I promised? What are you talking about?

WOMAN. Have you forgotten? Forgotten the night
  You drank with my father—

PEER.   If so, I've forgotten
  What I never knew. What's all this nonsense
  You're talking? When did we last meet?

WOMAN. We last met when we first met. [*To the* CHILD.]
  Give your father a drink. I think he's thirsty.

PEER. His father? You're drunk. Are you meaning to say—

WOMAN. Can't you recognize a pig by its skin?
  Where are your eyes? Can't you see he's lame
  In the leg, just as you're lame in the mind?

PEER. You'd have me believe—

WOMAN.   Are you trying to deny it?

PEER. This long-legged runt—!

WOMAN.   He is growing up fast.

PEER. Hag-face, don't father him on me!

WOMAN. That's enough, Peer Gynt, you uncouth ox!

                  [*Weeping.*]

Is it my fault that I'm not as pretty
As when you made love in the fields and woods?
When I was in labour in the autumn
The Devil supported my back for me;
Small wonder I've lost all the looks I had.
But if you would see me as I used to be
You have only to show that girl the door,
Pack her off out of sight and mind;
Do this, friend, and the hag-face will vanish.

PEER. Go away, troll-witch!

WOMAN.   You see if I do!

PEER. I'll smash your skull in!

WOMAN.   Dare to try!
Peer Gynt, I'm not so easily broken!
I shall come and visit you every day,
Push the door open and look inside.
When you're sitting with her beside the fire,
Fondling her, and kissing and loving,
I'll sit there, too, and claim my share.
She and I will take you in turns.
Farewell, dear friend; get married tomorrow!

PEER. You succubus!

WOMAN.   But I almost forgot!
You must bring up your child, you slippery rogue!—
Chip of the devil, will you go to your father?

CHILD [*spitting at him*]. I'll hack you with my axe: you wait!

WOMAN [*kissing the* CHILD]. What a head he has got on his shoulders!
You'll be just like your father when you grow up!

PEER [*stamping*]. I wish you as far away—

WOMAN.   As I'm near?

PEER [*wringing his hands*]. All of that!

WOMAN.   And it's all the result
Of dream and desire! I pity you.

PEER. It's still worse for another, for Solveig,
   My pure gold Solveig!

WOMAN.   The innocent
   Suffer, the devil says! His mother
   Whacked him because his father was drunk!

   [*She trudges off into the forest with the* CHILD, *who throws the ale-jug at*
   PEER.]

PEER [*after a long pause*]. The Boyg said: Go round and about.
   It looks this time as though I shall have to.
   My castle, which so nearly held her,
   Has come crashing down, and suddenly
   My world is ugly, and happiness over.
   Round and about, boy! There's no way
   Straight through this from you to her.
   Straight through? There ought to be a way.
   Isn't there a text about repentance?
   But what, now? How does it go? I've got
   No Bible, and most of it I forget,
   And there's no advice to be had in the forest.
   Repentance? But it might take years
   To win through. What a waste of life!
   To break what's vibrating and marvellous
   And try to piece it together again!
   You might do it to a fiddle, but not a bell.
   If you want green grass don't trample it down.
   Hallucination, that troll-witch business.
   It has disappeared now, out of sight.—
   Well, out of sight, but not out of mind.
   Skulking thoughts keep after me.
   Ingrid! The dancing three on the hill!
   Would they be there, too? Spitefully claiming
   To be hugged and held, like her, or gently
   Lifted, or touched with outstretched arms?
   Round and about, boy; if my arms
   Were as long as a fir-root or a pine-tree,
   I believe I should hold her too close even then
   To set her down clean and unharmed.—
   I've got to get round this, some way or other,

So that it's neither gain nor loss.
I must throw all this off, and try and forget it.

[*He goes a few steps towards the hut, but stops.*]

Go in now? So contaminated?
Go in with all this troll-dirt on me?
To speak, and say nothing: confess, yet conceal—?

[*He throws his axe aside.*]

It's Sunday evening. To go to her now,
In the state I am, would be sacrilege.

SOLVEIG [*in the doorway*]. Are you coming in?

PEER [*to himself*].   Round and about.

SOLVEIG. What did you say?

PEER.   You will have to wait.
It's beginning to get dark out here,
And there's something heavy I have to fetch.

SOLVEIG. I'll help you; we can lift it together.

PEER. No, stay where you are! I must bear it alone.

SOLVEIG. Not too far, then!

PEER.   You have to be patient;
Far or near, you must wait.

SOLVEIG [*nodding*].   I'll wait!

[PEER GYNT *goes down the forest path.* SOLVEIG *stands in the open half-door.*]

Sc. 4   _____

[AASE'S *cabin. Evening. A log fire is burning, lighting the chimney breast. A cat is on a chair by the foot of the bed.*
AASE *is in bed, plucking restlessly at the coverlet.*]

AASE. Oh, God, is he never coming?
Time drags along so slowly.
There's no one to send with a message;

And I've so much I must tell him.
No time to be lost! It has been
So sudden and unexpected.
Oh, if only I could be sure
That I wasn't too hard on him.

PEER [*entering*]. Good evening!

AASE.   God be praised!
You've got here, my dear, dear son!
You shouldn't have made the journey.
You risk your life coming here.

PEER. Ah, who cares about that?
I had to come here and see you.

AASE. Well, that puts Kari to shame;
Now I can go in peace.

PEER. Go? What nonsense is that?
Where are you thinking of going?

AASE. Ach, Peer, I'm reaching the end;
I haven't much longer now.

PEER [*turning awkwardly and crossing the room*].
I was trying to get out of the dark;
I thought I'd be free of it here—!
Are your feet and hands very cold?

AASE. Yes, Peer; it will soon be done.—
When you see my eyes cloud over
Close them with gentle fingers.
Remember to order a coffin,
Only, make sure it's a fine one.
Oh, but I had forgotten—

PEER.   Quiet, mother!
Time enough to think about that.

AASE. Yes, yes. [*She looks restlessly about the room.*]
                      You can see the little
They left. As you might have expected.

PEER [*awkward again*]. There you go! [*Harshly.*] I know I'm to blame.
But why do you have to remind me?

AASE. You! No, the cursed drink,
That's what made the disaster!
You had been drinking, my boy;
You didn't know what you were doing;
And you'd had that ride on the buck;
It's no wonder you lost your head!

PEER. Yes, well, let's drop the subject,
Try and forget all about it.
We'll leave any gloomy matters
Till later—some other day.

[*He sits on the edge of the bed.*]

Now, mother, we'll have a gossip,
But not about anything serious,—
Forget what's unpleasant and vexing,
The things that bruise and hurt us.
Why, look: the same old cat;
She's still keeping alive, then?

AASE. She carries-on so at night;
You know what that foretells!

PEER [*changing the subject*]. What's the news in the parish?

AASE [*smiling*]. They say somewhere about
Is a girl who longs for the mountains—

PEER [*hastily*]. How is Matt Moen getting on?

AASE. They say she pays no attention
To her mother and father's tears.
You ought to look in and see them;
You might be able to help—

PEER. And how is the blacksmith doing?

AASE. Don't mention that man to me.
I would rather tell you the name
Of the girl I was talking about—

PEER. No, now we'll have a gossip,
But not about anything serious,
Forget what's unpleasant and vexing,

    The things that bruise and hurt us.
    Are you thirsty? I'll get you a drink.
    Can you stretch out? The bed's a bit short.
    Let me see—I believe it's the one
    That I had when I was little!
    Remember, you used to sit
    In the evenings here beside me
    And tuck the fur-rug round me,
    And sing ballads and nursery-rhymes?

AASE. Yes, remember! Playing at sleigh-rides
    When your father was off on his travels.
    The coverlet was the sleigh-rug
    And the floor a frozen fjord.

PEER. Yes, but the best thing about it—
    Can you remember it, too?—
    Was all those marvellous horses—

AASE. Do you think I shall ever forget them?
    It was Kari's cat we had borrowed;
    It sat on the big log chair—

PEER. To the castle west of the moon
    And the castle east of the sun,
    To the Soria-Moria castle
    The road going up and down.
    You made a driving-whip
    From a stick we found in the cupboard.

AASE. I sat in the driving seat—

PEER. That's it; you let go the reins
    And kept turning round as we galloped
    To ask me if I was cold.
    God bless you, you old walnut,
    You were a lovable soul!—
    What are you groaning for?

AASE. My back; the planks feel hard.

PEER. Stretch out; I'll hold you up.
    There now, isn't that easier?

AASE [*uneasily*]. No, Peer, I want to move on.

PEER. Move on?

AASE.   Yes, to move on;
   I want it all the time now.

PEER. Nonsense! Let's pull up the coverlet.
   I'll sit here, the way you used to.
   We'll while the evening away
   With ballads and nursery-rhymes.

AASE. You'll find a book of sermons
   In the cupboard. My mind isn't easy.

PEER. In Soria-Moria Castle
   The King and the Prince are feasting.
   Lie back on the sledge-cushions;
   I'll drive you there over the moor—

AASE. But, kind son, am I invited?

PEER. Why yes, they've asked us both.

   [*He throws a cord round the chair where the cat is lying, takes a stick
   in his hand and sits at the foot of the bed.*]

   Gee-up! Get going, Black Beauty!
   You're not feeling cold, are you, mother?
   Gk, gk! What a speed we shall go
   When the grey gets into his stride!

AASE. Peer, what is it that's ringing?

PEER. The shining sleigh-bells, mother!

AASE. It seems such a hollow sound!

PEER. We're going over a fjord.

AASE. I'm afraid! A noise of rushing
   And sighing, a strange wild breath?

PEER. It's the pine-trees, mother, soughing
   In the meadows. You sit still.

AASE. That distant sparkle and flashing.
   All that light, where does it come from?

PEER. From the windows and doors of the castle.
  Can you hear them dancing?

AASE.   Yes.

PEER. St. Peter is standing outside
  Waiting to ask you in.

AASE. Is he greeting us?

PEER.   Very graciously,
  And pouring out sweet wine.

AASE. Wine? Are there cakes as well?

PEER. There are. A piled up plateful.
  And the dean's lamented wife
  Is preparing the coffee and afters.

AASE. Do you mean I'll be talking to her?

PEER. Just whenever you want to.

AASE. What a grand celebration to take
  A poor old creature like me to!

PEER [*cracking his whip*]. Gk, gk! Get a move on, Black Beauty!

AASE. Are you sure you're on the right road?

PEER [*cracking his whip again*]. The high road!

AASE.   The speed we're going
  Is beginning to make me tired.

PEER. I can see the castle ahead;
  We shall soon have finished the journey.

AASE. I'll lie back and close my eyes, then,
  And leave it to you, my son!

PEER. Come up, Greycoat, my spanker!
  There's a huge crowd. They're swarming
  Up to the gate of the castle.
  Here comes Peer Gynt with his mother!
  What's that, Mr. St. Peter?
  You won't let mother in?

You would have to search for years
To find someone as good.
We won't talk about me;
I'll turn back again at the gate.
I'd welcome a drink, if you offered;
If not, I'll set off with pleasure.
I've invented as many fibs
As the devil up in a pulpit,
And called my mother a hen
For keeping up such a cackle.
But just you respect and honour her
And make her feel at home.—
You'll find nobody better
Anywhere in the district.
Aha, so here's God the Father!
Now you're for it, St. Peter!

[*In a deep voice.*]

'Stop playing the heavy official:
Mother Aase will be my guest!'

[*He laughs loudly and turns to his* MOTHER.]

You see, as I thought it would be.
That's made him alter his tune.
[*Uneasily.*] What has happened to your eyes?
Mother! Have you gone mad—!

[*He goes to the head of the bed.*]

You mustn't lie there staring!
Say something; it's me, your son!

[*He feels her hands and brow cautiously; then throwing the cord back on the chair he says quietly.*]

That's it!—You can rest now, Greycoat;
The journey has come to an end.

[*He closes her eyes, and bends over her.*]

Take thanks for all you gave me,
The beatings and cradlesongs!—
And now you must thank me back—

[*He puts his cheek against her lips.*]

There; that was thanks for the ride.

KARI [*entering*]. What? Peer! You've come! So the worst
Of her grieving and longing is over!
God bless her, how soundly she's sleeping—
Or is she—

PEER.   Hush! she is dead.

[KARI *weeps beside the body.* PEER GYNT *paces up and down the room
for a time; at last he stops at the bedside.*]

PEER. Give my mother a decent burial.
I'm going away from here.

KARI. Are you going far?

PEER.   To the sea.

KARI. So far?

PEER.   And further still.

[*He goes.*]

ACT FOUR

The south-west coast of Morocco. A palm-grove. Under an awning, and standing on rush-matting, is a dinner-table, laid for a meal. In the grove behind are hammocks. Off shore, a steam-yacht flying the Norwegian and American flags. On the beach a jolly-boat. It is just before sunset.

PEER GYNT, *a handsome, middle-aged gentleman in an elegant travelling-suit, with gold-rimmed spectacles hanging from his waistcoat, is presiding at the head of the table.* MR. COTTON, MONSIEUR BALLON, HERR VON EBERKOPF, *and* HERR TRUMPETER-STRAALE *are finishing their dinner.*

PEER. Drink, gentlemen! If man is made
  To enjoy himself, enjoy yourselves.
  As somebody said: 'Lost is lost,
  And gone is gone.'—What can I pass you?

TRUMPETERSTRAALE. Dear Gynt, you're a superb host!

PEER. I divide the compliment between
  My money, my butler, and my cook.

COTTON. Right! Let's drink to the four of you!

BALLON. Monsieur, you possess a *gout*, a *ton*,
  Nowadays very seldom found
  In men living *en garçon*—
  A certain—how do you say?

VON EBERKOPF.   A touch
  Of emancipated soul-scrutiny,
  A cosmonopolyjudicobestriding,
  A vision breaching the cloud-barrier,
  Undeterred by narrow conformity:
  A characteristic of high discernment,
  An *Ur-natur* with life experience,
  Uniting the trilogy at the apex.
  Isn't that what you meant, monsieur?

BALLON. Yes, very possibly. It doesn't
   Sound so eloquent in French.

VON EBERKOPF. Ach, nein! Your language is so stiff.
   But if we wish to find the reason
   For this phenomenon—

PEER.   It's been found!
   The reason is that I'm not married.
   Yes, gentlemen, as obvious
   As that. What ought a man to be?
   Himself; there's my simple answer.
   His duty is to himself and what
   Is his. And how is this possible
   If he makes a pack-horse of himself
   For another person's benefit?

VON EBERKOPF. This for-and-within-yourself existence
   Incurred some struggle, I imagine—

PEER. Ah yes, indeed so, in the past;
   But I always came out of it with honour.
   Though on one occasion I came close
   To being trapped against my will.
   I was a lively, handsome fellow;
   And the lady I was attracted to
   Was of royal blood—

BALLON.   Of royal blood?

PEER [*casually*]. One of the ancient families,
   You know their kind—

TRUMPETERSTRAALE [*thumping the table*]. Blue-blooded trolls!

PEER [*shrugging his shoulders*].
   Obsolete aristocrats whose pride
   Is to see that no plebeian blot
   Is allowed to mar the family scutcheon.

COTTON. So nothing came of the affair?

BALLON. The family were against the match?

PEER. On the contrary.

BALLON.   Ah!

PEER [*picking his words*].   You see,
There were particular circumstances
That made it advisable to marry
As soon as we could. But, to be honest,
I found the whole thing, from first to last,
Very disagreeable. The truth is
I'm fastidious about certain things;
And I like to stand on my own feet.
So when my father-in-law hinted
That I'd have to change my name and status,
And apply for a nobleman's licence,
Together with other things I found
Unpalatable, not to say
Altogether unacceptable—
I turned down his ultimatum,
Surrendered up my young bride,
And withdrew gracefully.

[*He drums on the table portentously.*]

                    Ah, yes;
A destiny rules over us!
Humankind can depend on that,
And what a comfort it is to know it.

BALLON. And that brought the matter to an end?

PEER. No, no, I soon found otherwise;
Certain individuals
Kicked up a tremendous fuss about it,
The junior members of the family
Particularly. Seven of them
Challenged me to fight a duel.
That was a time I won't forget,
Though I came triumphantly out of it.
It cost blood; but still, that blood
Is evidence of my identity,
And points encouragingly towards
What I just now called the rule of destiny.

VON EBERKOPF. You have a view of life which puts you
  Into the category Thinker.
  Whereas the average intellect
  Separates the over-all scene
  Into detail, and ends in chaos,
  You manage to grasp the totality.
  You measure the whole by a single norm.
  You focus every random fact
  Until they become the radials
  Of a central life-philosophy.—
  And you've not been to a university?

PEER. No, as I believe I told you,
  I'm a plain, self-educated man.
  I've studied nothing methodically,
  But I have thought and speculated,
  And read, in a desultory way.
  I started somewhat late in life;
  When, as you know, it's rather a strain
  To plough through books, page after page,
  Trying to comprehend it all.
  I've a patchy knowledge of history,
  There's been no time for more than that.
  And as one needs something positive
  To depend on in times of stress,
  I've looked at religion from time to time.
  It goes down easier in small doses.
  A man shouldn't swallow all he reads,
  But rather choose what is useful to him.

COTTON. That's practical, I guess!

PEER [*lighting a cigar*].   Dear friends,
  Consider the rest of my career.
  What was I, when I came to the West?
  A poor boy, not a bean in the world.
  I had a struggle to keep alive;
  Believe me, I found it tough going.
  But life, my friends, is sweet, and death,
  As someone or other says, is bitter.
  Well! Luck, as you see, was on my side;

And our old friend Fate was accommodating.
I prospered. And, being adaptable,
I managed to get on better and better.
After ten years they nicknamed me
The Croesus of the Charleston traders.
My fame had spread from port to port;
And a fortune was piling up in the hold.

COTTON. What did you trade in?

PEER.   Very largely
  In negro-slaves for Carolina
  And heathen images for China.

BALLON. Fi donc!

TRUMPETERSTRAALE. Jesus, my dear Gynt!

PEER. It seems to you a market that hovers
  On the border-line of the permissible?
  I have felt the same myself, most keenly;
  I found it even odious.
  But, believe me, once begun
  It's very hard to break loose.
  And, of course, desperately complicated
  In the case of such a huge concern
  That gives employment to several thousands,
  To wind it up once and for all.
  Anyway, I don't really approve
  Of burning one's boats. On the other hand
  I've always had a great respect
  For what are known as the consequences;
  And the thought of overstepping the mark
  Has always made me a bit cautious.
  Besides, I'm not as young as I was,
  I was already approaching fifty—
  My hair was starting to turn grey;
  And, even though my health was excellent,
  The painful thought did occur to me:
  Who knows how soon the hour will strike
  When we shall have the jury's verdict
  And the goats be divided from the sheep.

P.G.—5

What could I do? To close the trade
With China was impossible.
However, I found a way. I started
Additional trading with that country.
In the spring I exported idols,
And in the autumn—missionaries,
Fully equipped with what they needed,
Such as stockings, bibles, rice and rum—

COTTON. All at a profit?

PEER.   Naturally!
With great success. They threw themselves
Heart and soul into the work.
For each idol sold, they baptized a coolie,
So the effect was neutralized.
The mission-field wasn't fallow a moment,
The missionaries had to wrestle with
An inexhaustible supply of idols.

COTTON. And what about the African shipments?

PEER. My ethics triumphed on this point, too.
I realized the traffic was wrong
For someone not in the prime of life.
You don't know when you may have to go.
What's more, there were a thousand traps
Laid by the philanthropic societies,
Not to mention acts of piracy
And the risks incurred by wind and weather.
These things combined to win the day.
I thought: Peter, trim your sails;
Take good care to mend your ways!
I bought some land in the South, and kept
The last cargo of flesh for myself,
Which happened to be a specially good one.
They throve, and got so sleek and fat
It was nice for me, and nice for them.
Yes, without boasting I can say
I behaved like a father to them,
Which paid excellent dividends.
I built schools, so that their morals

Should be maintained at a general level,
And I took good care the thermometer
Was never allowed to drop below it.
But I've given up the whole thing now,
Sold the plantation and the livestock,
Hair and hide. On the day I left
I gave every man, woman, and child
Free grog, and all of them got pickled:
And the widows got a supply of snuff.
So I trust—if the maxim 'He who does
No ill does good' is valid—then
I can be sure, more than most people,
That my past mistakes will be overlooked
And my virtues be seen to outweigh my sins.

VON EBERKOPF [*clinking glasses with him*].
How invigorating it is to hear
Of a life-principle put into practice
Released from the dark night of theory,
Uninfluenced by external protest!

PEER [*who has been steadily drinking*].
We Northerners understand the need
To fight our way through! The key to life
Is a simple one: to shut one's ears
To the invitation of the serpent.

COTTON. What kind of serpent is that, dear friend?

PEER. A small one, but full of wiles
To make a man commit himself.

[*He drinks again.*]

The whole art of taking risks,
Of having the strength of mind to act,
Is this: to keep your freedom of choice
Whatever traps life puts in your way,—
To know that other days will come
When the day of battle's over—
To know that behind you there is always
A bridge, if you have to beat a retreat.
This theory has carried me along

And coloured everything I did;
A theory I inherited
From childhood in my family home.

BALLON. You are Norwegian?

PEER. Yes, by birth.
But a world-citizen by nature.
For the good fortune I've enjoyed
I have to thank America.
I owe my well-stocked library
To the younger school of German writers.
From France I got my waistcoats, manners,
And what *esprit* I possess. From England
My industry, and a keen sense
Of what will be to my own advantage.
The Jew taught me how to wait.
A drop of *dolce far niente*   *SWEET DOING NOTHING*
Was imported to me from Italy,—
And once, in a very dangerous corner,
I defended myself with Swedish steel.

TRUMPETERSTRAALE [*raising his glass*].
Ah, Swedish steel!

VON EBERKOPF. First and foremost
We pay homage to the swordsman!

[*They clink glasses and drink with* PEER. *The drink is beginning to go to his head.*]

COTTON. All very good; but what I should like
To know, sir, is what you mean to do
With all your gold?

PEER [*smiling*]. Hm; do with it, eh?

ALL FOUR [*drawing closer*]. Yes, tell us!

PEER. Well, now; in the first place,
To travel. That's why I took you aboard
At Gibraltar, as travelling-companions.
I wanted a *corps de ballet* of friends
To dance around my Golden Calf.

VON EBERKOPF. Wittily said!

COTTON.   But no one ever
  Hoisted sail for the sake of sailing.
  You have a purpose, it seems to me.
  What is it?

PEER.   To be an Emperor.

GENTLEMEN. What?

PEER [*nodding*].   Emperor.

ALL FOUR.   Where?

PEER.   Of the whole world!

BALLON. And how, my friend?

PEER.   By the power of gold!
  It isn't a new idea; it's been
  The motive behind whatever I did.
  In childhood, I used to dream I soared
  On a cloud over the high seas,
  In royal robes, with a golden sword;—
  Till I came down again with a bump.
  But the goal, my friends, never wavered.—
  There's a text, I think, or someone said
  Somewhere, I can't remember where,
  That if you gained the whole world
  And lost your*self*, the gain would be
  A wreath on the forehead of a skull.
  That's the phrase, or something like it,
  And it isn't a mere flight of fancy.

VON EBERKOPF. But what *is* this Gyntian 'Self', exactly?

PEER. The world behind the curve of my brow
  Which demonstrates that I'm no one else
  But Me, as God is not the Devil.

TRUMPETERSTRAALE. Now I see what you're getting at!

BALLON. Sublime thinking!

VON EBERKOPF.   Highly poetic.

PEER [*with rising excitement*].
  The Gyntian 'Self'—it's the regiment
  Of wishes, appetites and desires;—
  The Gyntian 'Self' is the sea of ambitions,
  Needs and demands; in fact, whatever
  Causes my breast to heave uniquely,
  And makes me exist as the 'I' that I am.
  But just as the Almighty needs
  The earth to make him omnipotent,
  So, for my part, I need the gold
  To make myself an Emperor.

BALLON. But you have the gold!

PEER.   Not enough.
  Yes, for two or three days, maybe,
  As Emperor *à la* Lippe-Detmold.
  But I have to be myself *en bloc*—
  Gynt of the entire globe,
  Root and branch the sovereign Gynt!

BALLON [*enraptured*]. Possessing the world's supreme beauty!

VON EBERKOPF. The entire Johannesberger brewery!

TRUMPETERSTRAALE. All Charles the Twelfth's collection of weapons!

COTTON. Above all, a rewarding opportunity
  For trade—

PEER.   I've discovered that already;
  The result of anchoring in this harbour.
  This evening we shall be sailing north.
  The newspapers that came aboard
  Brought us some very important news—!

              [*He rises and lifts his glass.*]

  It seems good fortune never gives up
  Helping those with the will to take it—

GENTLEMEN. Well? Tell us!

PEER.   The Greeks are in revolt.

ALL FOUR [*springing to their feet*].
  What! The Greeks—?

PEER.   On their native soil.

ALL FOUR. Hurrah!

PEER.   And Turkey is in for trouble!

                [*He empties his glass.*]

BALLON. To Greece! The path to glory's open!
  I'll come to their help with a French sword!

VON EBERKOPF. I'll shout encouragement—from a distance!

COTTON. I'll make a deal in armaments!

TRUMPETERSTRAALE. Lead on! I shall find the spur-buckles
  Charles the Twelfth tore the Vizier's robe with!

BALLON [*embracing* PEER]. Forgive me, my friend; it seems I have been
  Misjudging you.

VON EBERKOPF [*shaking* PEER's *hand*]. Like *a dummkopf*
  I almost mistook you for a scoundrel!

COTTON. Too strong, that; merely for a fool!

TRUMPETERSTRAALE [*trying to kiss* PEER GYNT].
  I took you for a specimen
  Of the lowest kind of yankee hoodlum!
  Forgive me!

VON EBERKOPF. We were all confused—

PEER. What's all this about?

VON EBERKOPF.   Now we see,
  Marshalled in splendour, the complete
  Gyntian army of wishes, appetites
  And desires—

BALLON [*admiringly*]. So this is what it is
  To be Monsieur Gynt!

VON EBERKOPF [*likewise*]. To be
  Gynt with honour!

PEER.   Will you explain—

BALLON. You don't understand?

PEER.   I'm hanged if I do!

BALLON. How can that be? Aren't you setting
   Sail for Greece with a ship and money—?

PEER [*with contempt*]. No, thanks! I support the stronger side;
   I shall lend my money to the Turks.

BALLON. Impossible!

VON EBERKOPF.   Witty, but a joke!

PEER [*pausing, and leaning with dignity on a chair*].
   Well, gentlemen, I think it's better
   That we should part, before the last
   Ties of friendship go up in smoke.
   Who owns nothing can take a chance.
   If a man possesses not much more
   Than the strip of earth his shadow covers
   He can afford to be cannon-fodder.
   But if he stands on an eminence
   As I do, the stake's far higher.
   You go to Greece. I'll put you ashore
   And provide you all with weapons, gratis.
   The more you fan the flame of rebellion
   The better it will be for me.
   Strike your blow for freedom and right!
   Hurl yourselves in! Give the Turks hell;—
   And end your days gloriously
   Stuck on a Janizary's spear.—
   But count me out. [*He pats his pocket.*]
                    I've got money,
   And I'm *myself*—Sir Peter Gynt.

   [*He puts up his sunshade and walks into the grove where the hammocks
   can be seen.*]

TRUMPETERSTRAALE. The filthy cur!

BALLON.   No sense of honour!

COTTON. Oh, honour, that's neither here nor there;
   But think of the enormous profits
   If the country wins its independence—

BALLON. I saw myself as a liberator
   Surrounded by beautiful Greek women.

TRUMPETERSTRAALE. I saw, held in my Swedish hands,
   Those legendary spur-buckles!

VON EBERKOPF. I saw the fatherland's vast culture
   Spreading across earth and sea—!

COTTON. It's the financial loss that's worst.
   Goddammit! I could cry my eyes out!
   I saw myself owning Olympus.
   If that mountain's like its reputation
   There must be copper there, which ought
   To be dug out. And furthermore,
   There's this river Castalia
   People talk so much about,
   With one waterfall after another:
   That, at the lowest estimate,
   Should be good for more than a thousand horse-power—!

TRUMPETERSTRAALE. I shall still go! My Swedish sword
   Has greater value than Yankee gold!

COTTON. Maybe; but crowded in the ranks
   We'll be trampled underfoot by the mob;
   And what profit do you see in that?

BALLON. *Merde!* So near the peak of success,
   Only to have to watch it buried.

COTTON [*shaking his fist towards the yacht*].
   Locked up there, in that black chest,
   Is the nabob's nigger-sweating gold!

VON EBERKOPF. A masterly thought! Quick! Let's go!
   His empire is about to fall!
   Hurrah!

BALLON.   What now?

VON EBERKOPF.   We seize power!
  The crew can easily be bribed.
  Aboard! I'll commandeer the yacht!

COTTON. You'll—what?

VON EBERKOPF.   I'll grab the whole concern!

[He goes down to the jolly-boat.]

COTTON. My own interests seem to dictate
  I should grab as well.

[He follows.]

TRUMPETERSTRAALE.   What a vulture!

BALLON. Villainous behaviour! Still—enfin!

[He follows the others.]

TRUMPETERSTRAALE. What else can I do but follow suit—
  But I protest to all the world!

[He goes after them.]

Sc. 2 _____

*[Another part of the coast. Moonlight and drifting clouds. The yacht
is far out at sea, under full steam.*
    PEER GYNT *runs along the shore, now pinching himself awake, now
gazing out over the ocean.]*

PEER. Nightmare!—Illusion!—I'll wake up soon!
  She's moving off shore! At the rate of knots!
  Sheer illusion! I'm asleep, or delirious!

[He wrings his hands.]

It can't be that I'm going to die!

[He tears his hair.]

A dream! It has to be a dream!
Horrible! But obviously true!
My arse-licking friends! Hear me, God!
You're an all-wise and righteous judge!

[*With upstretched arms.*]

It's me, Peer Gynt! Protect me, God!
Take care of me, Father, or I shall perish!
Make them back the engine! And lower the boat!
Stop the thieves! Tangle the rigging!
Listen! Don't fret about other people!
The world can look after itself for a while!—
He's not hearing me! Stone deaf, as usual!
What a set-up! A God who's run out of advice!

[*He signals to the sky.*]

Pst! I've got rid of the nigger-plantation!
I've sent missionaries to Asia! Doesn't
One good turn deserve another?
Get me on that boat!

[*A sheet of flame shoots skywards from the yacht, followed by smoke and an explosion.* PEER GYNT *gives a cry and sinks on to the sand. Gradually the smoke clears; the ship has vanished.*]

PEER [*low-voiced and pale*]. The sword of the Lord!
Every man and mouse gone plumb to the bottom!
Thank God for a lucky accident!—
[*With emotion.*] Accident? No, it was more than that.
I was *meant* to be saved, and they to perish.
Thanks and praise that you kept me safe,
Preserved me in spite of all my faults—

[*He takes a deep breath.*]

What marvellous peace and consolation
To know you are personally looked after.
But in this desert! Where's food and water?
Oh, I'll find something. He will provide.
There's no danger;—[*Loudly and ingratiatingly.*]
                    He won't allow
A poor little sparrow like me to perish!
Practise humility. And give Him time.
Rest in the Lord, and don't be cast down.

[*With a leap of terror.*]

Was that a lion growling in the rushes?

[*His teeth chattering.*]

No, it wasn't a lion. [*Plucking up courage.*]
            A lion; is it likely?
Wild animals like to stay at a distance.
Faced with their overlords they're wary.
It's instinctive; they feel, quite rightly,
It's risky to play with elephants.—
But still, I'd better look for a tree.
Here's a grove of acacias and palms;
If I climb up there I'll be safe and protected,—
Particularly if I can remember
A psalm or two—[*He climbs a tree.*]
            Morning is certainly
Different from evening. That text has given
Men food for thought often enough.

[*He settles himself comfortably.*]

How good to feel the spirit uplifted.
Virtuous thoughts are better than riches.
Simply trust in Him. He knows
Just how much of the cup of affliction
I have the stamina to drink.
He's paternally disposed towards me;—

[*He looks out to sea, and whispers with a sigh:*]

But economical—no, he's not that!

_____

[*Night. A Moorish camp on the edge of the desert.* SOLDIERS *resting round the camp fires.* A SLAVE *runs on, tearing his hair.*]

SLAVE. The Emperor's white charger has vanished!

[*A* SECOND SLAVE *runs on, tearing his clothes.*]

2ND SLAVE. The Emperor's sacred robes have been stolen!

GUARD [*entering*]. A hundred lashes on the soles of the feet
For anyone failing to catch the thief!

[*The* SOLDIERS *mount their horses and gallop off in all directions.*]

[*Dawn. The grove of acacias and palms.* PEER GYNT *in the tree with a broken branch in his hands, trying to beat off a horde of* MONKEYS.]

PEER. Disaster! A most unpleasant night. [*Swiping:*]
   Are you back again? This is bloody hell!
   Throwing fruit at me. No, something else.
   Your Barbary ape's a loathsome animal!
   It's written: 'Watch and keep up the fight!'
   I'm damned if I can. I'm shagged out.

[*They attack him again. Desperately.*]

I must put a stop to this persecution!
I must try and catch one of the brutes,
Hang him and skin him, and disguise
Myself, somehow, in his hairy coat.
And perhaps the others will think I'm genuine.—
What is a man? Only dust.
He has to make some concession to fashion.—
Another onslaught! They're swarming like bees.
Buzz off! Shoo! They're going berserk.
If I'd only got a false tail to wear,—
Or something to make me look like an animal—
What now? Something scrambling over head—

[*He looks up.*]

The grandfather—with a paw full of filth—!

[*He crouches apprehensively, quite still for a moment. The ape moves.* PEER *starts to wheedle and coax him as if he were a dog.*]

Hey, are you there, good old Buster?
There's a nice fellow. He wants to be friendly!
He won't throw anything; of course he won't—
This is me! Diggy-diggy! We're splendid friends!
Wough-wough! You see, I speak your language.
We both belong to the same family!—
Buster shall have some sugar presently!—
The beast! The whole load on top of me!
Ugh, this is disgusting!—Or was it
Food? The taste might have been anything;
With taste, it's a question of what you're used to.

What philosopher was it who said:
Spit, and hope to acquire the habit?—
Here are the young ones! [*Lashing out at them.*]
                                        It's monstrous
That a man, one of the Lords of Creation,
Should be compelled to—! Murder! Murder!
The old one was hideous, but these are worse!

Sc.5 —————

[*Early morning. A stony place overlooking the desert. A cave and a ravine at one side.*

A THIEF *and* A FENCE *are in the ravine with the Emperor's horse and robes. The horse, richly caparisoned, is tied to a rock. Horsemen can be seen in the distance.*]

THIEF.	The tongues of the lances Are licking, flickering,— Watch out, watch out!
FENCE.	My noddle already Is rolling in the sand, Alas, alas!
THIEF [*folding his arms*].	My dad was a thief, So his son has to be one.
FENCE.	Mine was a fence, So I'm a fence, too.
THIEF.	You have to put up With the person you are.
FENCE [*listening*].	Steps in the scrub! We must fly! But where?
THIEF.	The cavern is deep And the Prophet great!

[*They make off, leaving their booty behind. The horsemen in the distance disappear.*]

PEER [*enters, cutting a whistle from a reed*].
What a miraculous hour of the morning!

The dung-beetle trundles his ball in the dust;
The snail has come to the door of his shell.
First light; yes, it has gold in its mouth.—
Nature gives an astonishing power
To the light of day, there's no doubt of that.
You feel so safe, your courage rising,
Prepared to tackle a bull if you have to.
Such quiet! The joy of the open country,—
It's strange I have always despised it before;
And that men should crowd themselves in a city,
To be merely elbowed out of the door.—
Oh, look—there's a quicksilver lizard,
Snatching without a thought in its head.
What innocence, even in the animals.
Each obeys its Creator, unquestioning,
Keeping its own indelible character,
Playing or fighting, always itself,
As it was when God said 'Let there be life'.

[He puts his spectacles on his nose.]

A toad. In the middle of a block of sandstone.
In a fossil world. Just his head showing.
He sits and looks out at the world
As though through a window: himself—sufficient. *[Reflects.]*
Sufficient? Himself?—Where does that come from?
Something I read when I was a boy.
In the family prayer-book? Or the Wisdom of Solomon?
It's hopeless; I notice as time goes by
I'm losing my memory for dates and places.

[He sits in the shade.]

Here's a cool place, to stretch out and rest in.
Ferns; and these look like edible roots.

[He tastes one.]

More suitable for animal food.—
Well, they say 'You must master your instincts'!
And, furthermore, 'subdue your pride'.
Also, 'the humble shall be exalted'.

[*Uneasily.*]

Exalted? I'm sure that will happen to me;—
Anything else is unthinkable.
Fate will get me out of this place
And find me a way to begin again.
I'm being tried; salvation comes later,—
If only God will keep me healthy.

[*He shakes off these thoughts, lights a cigar, stretches himself, and stares out over the desert.*]

What a huge, limitless wilderness.—
Away over there, a striding ostrich.
What sense can you make of God's purpose
In all this emptiness and death?
There's nothing life-giving anywhere here,
A charred place, no good to anyone;—
A slice of world, eternally sterile;
A corpse that never, since earth was,
Gave a gesture of thanks to its maker,—
Why was it made?—Nature's prodigal.—
Is that the sea, glittering and flashing
Over in the east? Impossible!
It must be a mirage. The sea's to the west;
Higher up behind me, dammed
Off from the desert by a slope of dunes.

[*A thought strikes him.*]

Dammed off?—Now, why couldn't I
The slope is quite shallow. Dammed off!
It only needs one break, a canal,—
A flood of life would come cascading
Down through the gap, and fill the desert!
Soon the whole of this burning grave
Would be like a fresh, rippling sea.
Oases would lift from the water like islands,
Mount Atlas be green as the northern shore,
And ships would skim, like careening birds,
Southward along the caravan tracks.
A living air would scatter this torpid

Vapour, and the clouds drop dew;
Men would build city after city,
And grass grow under the waving palms.
The land south of the Sahara
Would be the shores of a new culture.
Steam would drive the factories
Of Timbuctoo, and Bornu would be
Colonized in a matter of weeks.
Archaeologists would drive their wagons
Safely through Habès to the Upper Nile.
On a plump oasis in the ocean
I would propagate the Norwegian race;
A dalesman's blood is almost royal,
And, crossed with an Arab, would do the trick.
Overlooking the bay on rising ground
I shall build the chief city, Peeropolis.
The world's outmoded! Now it's the turn
Of Gyntiana, my new young land!

[*He leaps up.*]

Given the capital, it's already done.—
A golden key to the gate of the ocean!
A crusade against Death! That old skinflint
Can open the sack he sits brooding over.
Because Freedom is the trumpet call
In every land; like Noah's donkey
I'll send a cry across the world,
Baptize the lands now under a yoke
In the name of freedom and the golden future.
I must forage east and west for the money!
My kingdom—half my kingdom for a horse!

[*The horse whinnies in the ravine.*]

A horse! And robes! And jewels—and weapons!

[*He goes closer.*]

Impossible! Yes, real! I've read
Somewhere that faith can move mountains;—
But fancy it shifting a horse as well—!

Absurd! But, no fooling, the horse is here;—
Ab esse ad posse, and all the rest of it—

FROM TO BE TO TO BE ABLE TO

[He puts on the robes and looks down at himself.]

Sir Peter,—and a Turk from top to toe!
Well, you never know what will happen to you.—
Gk, gk!—Come up, my galloping grey!

[He climbs into the saddle.]

Gold stirrups, too, for my feet to go in!—
You can tell who's well-born by the bloodstock they ride!

[He gallops into the desert.]

Sc. 6

[The tent of an Arab Sheik, standing alone in an oasis. PEER GYNT, *in his eastern robes, reclines on cushions. He is drinking coffee and smoking a long pipe.* ANITRA *and a group of* GIRLS *are dancing and singing for him.]*

CHORUS OF GIRLS. The Prophet is come!
    The Prophet, the lord, the all-knowing,
    To us, to us he has come
    Riding over the sand!
    The Prophet, the lord, the infallible,
    To us, to us he has come
    Sailing over the sand.
    Sound the flute and drum;
    The Prophet, the Prophet is come!

ANITRA. His stallion is milk-white
    Like the rivers of Paradise.
    Bow, every knee and head!
    His eyes are dancing stars.
    No human can endure
    The glowing of that fire.
    Across the desert he came.
    From his breast sprang pearls and gold.
    The darkness of simoom
    And drought lay all behind him;
    Light was where he rode.

He, the unexampled,
Came across the desert
Arrayed like a son of the earth.
Kaba, Kaba stands empty;—
He himself proclaims it!

GIRLS. Sound the flute and drum;
The Prophet, the Prophet is come!

[*The* GIRLS *dance to soft music.*]

PEER. I have seen it in print—and it's very true—
'No one's a prophet in his own country.'—
It's certainly better being here
Than back among those Charleston traders.
There was something hollow in all that,
Something alien to me, something
Dubious lurking in the background.
I was never at home in such a set-up,
And never really the man for the job.
What was I doing in that galère?
Rummaging in the garbage of trade.
When I think of it now, I don't understand;—
It just happened; that's all there is to it.
To be yourself on the basis of gold
Is like trying to build a house on sand.
People go down on their knees in the dirt
When they see your rings and your gold watch;
They lift their hats to a diamond tie-pin;
But the rings and things aren't the man himself.—
A prophet; now there the position is clearer.
You know at least what footing you're on.
If you prosper, it's you—not your pounds,
Shillings and pence—that gets the applause.
You are what you are, and no nonsense;
You're not indebted to luck or chance,
You don't have to depend on orders and contracts.—
A prophet; yes, that's the thing for me.
And it caught me totally unaware—
Simply by loping across the desert
And coming across these children of nature.

The Prophet had come; they made that clear.
I didn't mean to deceive them;—answering
Prophetwise isn't really lying;
And, anyhow, I can always resign.
I'm not committed; it might have been worse;—
Just a private matter, you could call it;
I can go as I came; my horse stands ready;
In short, I'm master of the situation.

ANITRA [*approaching from the entrance*]. Prophet and master!

PEER.   What would you have,
My slave?

ANITRA.   Outside the sons of the desert
Are begging to look upon your face.

PEER. Tell them to go and stand at a distance;
Tell them I hear prayers miles away.
And add: I won't have men in here!
Men are a worthless lot, my child,—
Bad-tempered rascals, for the most part!
Anitra, you can't think how vilely
They have swind— I mean, have sinned, my child!
Enough of that! Dance for me, women!
The Prophet wants to forget the past.

GIRLS [*dancing*]. The Prophet is good; the Prophet is grieved
For the evil done by the sons of dust!
The Prophet is meek; praise to his meekness;
He opens Paradise for sinners!

PEER [*his eyes following* ANITRA *during the dance*].
Her feet move like the patter of drums.
Hey! She is exquisite, this filly.
Her build is on the generous side,
Not what beauty normally measures;
But what is beauty? A pure convention,—
Value depends on where and when.
The extravagance is very pleasing
When you've had a bellyfull of the normal.
The usual recipe has no kick.

No: either very plump, or very skinny;
Indecently young or incredibly old;—
The in-between is a drag on the spirit.
Her feet aren't altogether clean,—
Nor her arms, either; especially one.
But that isn't a serious drawback.
I'd rather say it was in her favour—
Anitra, listen!

ANITRA [*approaching*]. Your slave hears you!

PEER. You attract me, child! The Prophet is touched.
If you don't believe me, I'll prove it to you;—
I will make you a houri in Paradise!

ANITRA. Impossible, master!

PEER.   Do you think I'm joking?
I'm perfectly serious, as I'm alive!

ANITRA. But I haven't a soul.

PEER.   Then you'll have to get one!

ANITRA. But how, master?

PEER.   Leave it to me;—
I shall take your education in hand.
No soul? I've noticed, to my regret,
You appear to be a bit dumb, as they say.
But, tush; there's always room for a soul.
Come here! Let me measure your cerebellum.—
There's room; there's room; I thought there was.
It's true, it will never go very deep;
You mustn't expect a *large* soul;—
But that's nothing to worry about;—
You will have enough not to feel embarrassed.

ANITRA. The prophet is good—

PEER.   Are you hesitating?

ANITRA. I would rather—

PEER.   Don't be afraid to speak.

ANITRA. I don't mind about the soul so much;—
I'd rather have—

PEER.   What?

ANITRA [*pointing at his turban*]. That wonderful opal!

PEER [*enchanted, as he gives her the jewel*].
Anitra! You true daughter of Eve!
You affect me like a magnet.
I'm a man. To quote a famous author:
'Das ewig weibliche ziehet uns an!'

Sc. 7   ——————

[*A moonlit night. The palm-grove outside* ANITRA's *tent.*
    PEER GYNT, *with an Arabian lute in his hand, is sitting under a
tree. His beard and hair have been trimmed; he looks much younger.*]

PEER [*playing and singing*].
                I locked the gates of paradise
                    And took the key in my keeping.
                And carried by the northern breeze
                I sailed away across the seas
                    And left the women weeping.

                Southward, southward the keel cut
                    The salt waves through like wire.
                And where the palm-trees proudly sway
                In a green garland round the bay
                    I set my ship on fire.

                I climbed aboard a desert ship,
                    A four-legged ship was he.
                It foamed under the lash's gird;—
                    I am a migratory bird
                    Carolling on a tree!

                Anitra, nectar of the palm;
                    This much I will allow!
                Angora goatmilk cheese, or fish,
                    Is not as edible a dish,
                    Anitra dear, as thou!

[He hangs the lute over his shoulder and moves towards the tent.]

A silence! Is my charmer listening?
Has she heard my serenade?
Is she peering round the curtain,
Veil, and all the rest, abandoned?—
Hear that? A sound as though a cork
Had exploded from a bottle!
There it was again! And there!
Sighing of love? Surely, singing;—
No, unquestionably snoring.—
Sweet harmony! Anitra sleeps.
Nightingale, hold your tongue!
Woe betide you if you wake her
With your jug-tereu-tereu—
Ah well, forget it, as they say!
The nightingale is a born singer;
And so am I, if it comes to that.
He ensnares all hearts, as I do,
Tender, gentle hearts, with music.
This cool night was made for singing;
Song is the element we share;
We become ourselves in singing,
We, Peer Gynt and the nightingale.
The simple fact of a girl sleeping
Is the climax of my passion;—
Touching with my parted lips
The rim of the glass, not drinking yet;—
But, by heaven, here she is!
After all, that's really better.

ANITRA [*from the tent*]. Master, do you call in the night?

PEER. Yes, indeed; the prophet calls.
  I was awakened by the cat
  Giving a wild hunting-cry—

ANITRA. Not a hunting-cry, my lord;
  Far worse than that.

PEER.   What was it, then?

ANITRA. Have mercy—

PEER.   Tell me!

ANITRA.   It makes me blush—

PEER [*approaching her*].
    Was it, perhaps, the same emotion
    That completely overwhelmed me
    When I gave my opal to you?

ANITRA [*horrified*]. Compare you, treasure of the world,
    With a horrible old cat!

PEER.   My child,
    Looked at from the point of view
    Of love-making, tom-cat and prophet
    In the end are much the same.

ANITRA. Master, the honey of a jest
    Flows from your lips.

PEER.   My little friend,
    You judge great men, as all girls do,
    On appearances. Fundamentally
    I'm a humorous chap, especially
    In a duologue. But my position
    Makes me assume a mask of gravity.
    My official duties make me stern;
    All the responsibility
    Of coping with everybody's troubles
    Turns me into a Jeremiah;
    But it's only on the tongue.—
    Enough of this! When we're together
    I'm Peer—well, I am who I am.
    Suppose we now forget the prophet;
    You have me here, myself in person.

    [*He sits under a tree and draws her to him.*]

    Come, Anitra, we'll relax
    Under the palm's green fan! And I
    Will whisper while you smile, and then
    Vice versa presently;
    You will whisper words of love
    To me, and I shall do the smiling.

ANITRA [*lying at his feet*].
  Each word you say is like a song,
  What I can understand of it.
  Master, tell me, can a daughter
  Get a soul by listening?

PEER. Soul, the intellect's light and reach,
  You shall have all in good time.
  When the east writes characters
  Gold on rose to spell the day,
  You shall have your first instruction
  And see how well I educate you.
  But in this magic mood of night
  I should be certifiable
  If I served up dreary scraps
  Of knowledge like a schoolmaster.
  Anyway, if you work it out,
  The soul's not the important thing.
  The heart is what concerns us most.

ANITRA. Speak, O master! When you speak
  I catch gleams of light, like opals!

PEER. Too much intelligence is folly;
  Coward blossoms into tyrant;
  The truth, when it's overdone,
  Is wisdom standing on its head.
  Yes,—I'd be a liar to say
  There aren't well-fed souls on earth
  Who're never going to get things clear.
  I once knew a man like that,
  One in a thousand; and even he
  Managed to mistake his way,
  Lost the meaning in the shouting.—
  You see the desert round this place?
  I only have to wave my turban,
  And I could force the entire ocean
  To tip over and fill the lot.
  But I'd be an idiot to start
  Creating seas and continents.
  D'you know what living is?

  P.G.—6

ANITRA.   Teach me.

PEER. To live is to be borne along
    Dryshod on the river of time
    Absolutely as yourself.
    Only as total man can I be
    What I really am, my sweet one!
    Old eagles drop their feathers,
    Old fogeys shuffle and stoop,
    Old crones lose their teeth,
    Old misers have shrivelled hands,—
    And all of them have withered souls.
    Youth! Youth! I mean to dominate
    Like a burning, absolute sultan,—
    Not on the shores of Gyntiana
    Under the vine-leaves and the palm-trees,—
    But in the fresh lap of the virgin
    Thoughts of a woman.—Do you see now,
    Little fish, why I've graciously
    Charmed you, chose *your* heart, established
    There, if I may so describe it,
    My whole nature's Caliphate?
    All your desires belong to me.
    I'm a demagogue in love!
    You are going to be mine only.
    I am what has to dazzle you
    As if I were gold or precious stones.
    If we part, life is over,—
    Yours, at any rate, take note!
    I must be sure that every inch
    And fibre of you, without a will
    For yea or nay, is full of me.
    Your shadowy coils of midnight love,
    All the charms that can be named,
    Like the gardens of Babylon
    Will beckon me to a Sultan's bed.
    And so really your empty head
    Is no bad thing. When he has a soul
    A person gets too self-absorbed.
    And, listen, while we're on the subject;

If you want it, you can gladly
Have an anklet of silver bells;—
It works out well for both of us;
I'll take the place of a soul for you,
And all the rest is—status quo.

[ANITRA *snores.*]

What? She's asleep. Has everything
That I've been saying been chucked away?—
No; it only confirms the power
I have, that she should float along
In dreams on the stream of my love-talk.

[*He gets up and puts jewels in her lap.*]

Here are brooches! And more yet!
Sleep, Anitra! Dream of Peer—
Sleep! By sleeping you have put
A crown on to your Emperor's head!
A conquest of personality
Is what Peer Gynt has achieved tonight.

SL. 8 —————————

[*A caravan route. The oasis can be seen in the far distance.*
    PEER GYNT, *on his white horse, is galloping through the desert,
    with* ANITRA *in front of him on the saddle-bow.*]

ANITRA. Stop it, or I'll bite you!

PEER.   Little rogue!

ANITRA. What do you want?

PEER.   To play doves and eagles!
    To carry you off! To make merry hell!

ANITRA. For shame! An old prophet like you—

PEER.   Nonsense!
    The Prophet isn't old, you goose!
    Does this look like old age to you?

ANITRA. Let me be! I want to go home!

PEER. You flirt! Go home! To father-in-law!
  Charming! We've escaped like wild birds
  Out of the cage; we must never darken
  His doors again. Besides, one should never
  Stay too long in the same place.
  Familiarity breeds contempt;—
  Especially when you come as a prophet
  Or something of that sort. A fleeting
  Appearance, and then away like a song.
  It's high time my visit came to an end.
  They're fickle souls, these sons of the desert;—
  The incense and prayers had petered out.

ANITRA. But are you a prophet?

PEER.   I'm your Emperor!

[*He tries to kiss her.*]

  There's a preening little woodpecker!

ANITRA. Give me the ring on your finger.

PEER.   Take it,
  Anitra love, and the rest of the baubles!

ANITRA. Your words are songs! They hang on my ear!

PEER. It's heavenly to be loved so much.
  I'll dismount, and lead the horse like your slave!

[*He gives her the riding crop and dismounts.*]

  There now, my rose, my lovely flower;
  I'll trudge along in the sand beside you
  Until I get a well-deserved sunstroke.
  I'm young, Anitra; don't forget it!
  Don't take what I do too seriously.
  Playing the fool is a sign of youth!
  If your understanding wasn't so dense
  You would know, my elegant oleander,
  Your lover is fooling—therefore, he's young!

ANITRA. All right, you are young. Have you any more rings?

PEER. Aren't I? There; catch! I can leap like a stag!
 If there had been any vine-leaves here
 I'd have made a wreath to put on my head.
 By God, I'm young! I'll have a dance!

[*Dancing and singing.*]

> I'm a blessed cockerel!
> Peck me, my pullet,
> While I pirouette it!
> I'm a blessed cockerel!

ANITRA. You're sweating, my Prophet; I'm afraid you'll melt;
 Let me carry that heavy bag for you.

PEER. What a kind thought! Carry it always;—
 When you're in love, who cares about gold?

[*Dancing and singing again.*]

> Scalliwag Peer
> He doesn't know where
> To put his feet
> Because life is sweet
> For scalliwag Peer!

ANITRA. Such delight, when the prophet dances!

PEER. To hell with the prophet!—Let's swap clothes!
 Come on! Get out of them!

ANITRA.   Your kaftan
 Would be too long, your belt too big,
 Your stockings too tight for me!

PEER.   Eh bien!

[*He kneels.*]

 Make me suffer intensely, then;—
 When you're in love pain is welcome!
 Listen, when we get back to my castle—

ANITRA. To your paradise;—how far away?

PEER. Oh, a thousand miles—

ANITRA.   Too far!

PEER.   But, listen;—
You'll be getting that soul I promised you—

ANITRA. Thanks; I'll manage without a soul.
But you want to suffer—

PEER [*getting up*].   By thunder, I do!
Intense, but short—say, two or three days!

ANITRA. Anitra obeys the prophet!—Farewell!

> [*She raps him hard across the knuckles and dashes at full gallop back through the desert.*]

PEER [*standing for a long time thunderstruck*].
Well, may I be ——!

Sc. 9   ——————

> [*The same place, an hour later.*
>   PEER GYNT, *soberly and thoughtfully, is stripping off his Turkish robes, bit by bit. At last he takes his little travelling-cap out of his coat pocket, and stands once again in his European dress.*]

PEER [*throwing his turban far away from him*].
There lies the Turk, and here stand I!—
Acting the heathen doesn't work.
Lucky it was just a matter of costume,
And not heredity, as they say.—
What was I doing in such a set-up?
It serves you best to live like a Christian,
Not peacock about in fancy costume:
To base your actions on law and morality,
Be your true self, and win in the end
A graveside speech, and wreaths on your coffin.

> [*He walks a few steps.*]

That bitch;—she came within an ace
Of making me lose my head altogether.
I should be a troll if I could make out
What fuddled and confused me so.

Ah well; it's a good thing it's over!
If the joke had gone on another minute
I should have looked ridiculous.—
I made a mistake. It's some consolation
That the error was due to my false position.
I wasn't the person responsible.
It was really the routine life of a prophet,
So utterly lacking the salt of activity,
That took its revenge in these lapses of taste.
Being a prophet is a horrible business!
Your duty's to wrap yourself in a mist;
You finish your chances as a prophet
The moment you start behaving sensibly.
And so I was merely doing my job
When I made pretty speeches to that goose.
Nevertheless—[*He bursts out laughing.*]
          To think of it!
I tried to make time stand still by dancing!
To reverse the tide by prancing about!
Playing the lute, hugging and sighing,
And I end up plucked like a cockerel.
Religious fervour with a vengeance!
Yes, plucked!—And plucked to the wide!
Well, I've still got something in reserve;
Some in America, a bit in my pocket;
I'm not down on my uppers yet.—
And the middle of the road is the best position.
I'm not cluttered with a horse and a coachman;
No transport or luggage to worry about;
In short, I'm master of the situation.
Which way shall I choose? Of all the many
Possibilities? Choice is how
You can tell an intelligent man from a fool.
My business career is a closed chapter;
My love-life is a cast-off garment.
I won't go backwards like a crab.
'Forward or back, it's the same distance;
'Out or in, it's equally narrow',—
As I once read in some high-flown article.—
So now something new; a great enterprise;

A purpose worth the money and effort.
What if I write my life story,
Keeping nothing back,—a book that will set
A fine example, a guide to living?—
Or, wait! I've all the time in the world;—
Suppose, as a well-travelled scholar,
I studied the whole glut of the ages!
Yes, yes; *that's* the thing for me!
I read enough legends when I was small,
And I've kept it up, more or less, ever since.—
I'll record the progress of the human race!
I'll float like a feather on the stream of history,
Make it live again, as though in a dream,—
See the heroes battling for power and right,
As an onlooker, from a safe distance,—
Watch thinkers perish, and martyrs bleed,
Watch kingdoms rise and kingdoms fall,—
Great epochs growing from small beginnings;
In short, skim off the cream of history.—
I must try to get hold of a copy of Becker,
And go through it chronologically,
As far as I can.—Of course it's true
That I haven't much grounding in the subject,
And history's inner workings are subtle;—
But when the starting-point is weakest
The result is often the most original.—
Marvellous to have such a task in hand
And plunge right through it, like flint or steel!

[*With quiet emotion.*]

To sever the ties that are holding you
On every side to home and friends,—
Blow all your worldly goods sky-high,—
Bid a fond farewell to the pleasures of love,—
All to discover the clue to Truth.—

[*He wipes a tear from his eye.*]

That's what makes the authentic inquirer!—
I feel immeasurably happy.
I have solved the riddle of my destiny.

I must stick to it now through thick and thin!
It's excusable to hold up my head
And be proud of being the man Peer Gynt,
Alias: the Emperor of Human Experience.—
I shall have the absolute key to the past;
No longer have to cope with the living;
The present isn't worth an old boot;
The conduct of men is perverse and gutless;
No wings to their spirits, no weight to their deeds;—

[*He shrugs his shoulders.*]

And women,—there's a flimsy collection!

[*He goes.*]

Sc. 10 _____

[*A summer's day. Far in the north. A hut in the deep forest. The door, with a big wooden bar, stands open. Reindeer antlers above the door. A flock of goats by the wall of the hut.*

A middle-aged woman, fair-haired, beautiful, sits spinning in the sun.]

THE WOMAN [*gazing down the pathway as she sings*].
    Winter may go, and spring appear,
    Next summer pass, and all the year.
    And yet a time there *will* be, when
    My love is in my arms again.

[*She calls the goats, and returns to her singing and spinning.*]

    God bless you in your journeying,
    And to his peace your spirit bring.
    Here shall I wait until my end,
    Or meet with you in heaven, friend.

Sc. 11 _____

[*In Egypt. Dawn. The statue of Memnon rising out of the sand.*
PEER GYNT *wanders in, and gazes round him.*]

PEER. Here's a good place to begin my wanderings.—
Now I'm Egyptian for a change;

But Egyptian based on the Gyntian ego.
Later, I'll make my way to Assyria.—
If I start with the first day of creation
It's bound to end in total disaster;—
I shall side-step Biblical history;
Its secular traces I'll come across everywhere;
But to go into its details thoroughly
Lies outside my province and my powers.

[*He sits on a stone.*]

I'll sit in patience, and wait for the statue
To sing its usual hymn to sunrise.
And after breakfast I'll climb the pyramid;
If there's time, I can look at the inside later.
Then by land I'll follow the Red Sea;
Perhaps I can find King Potiphar's grave.—
An Asiatic, in Babylon
I'll look about to find the famous
Hanging Gardens and the whores:
The chief traces of culture, in fact.
And then at one bound to the Trojan walls.
From Troy there's a direct sea-route
Across to the glory that was Athens;—
There, stone by stone, on the actual spot,
I'll survey the pass that Leonidas guarded;—
I'll acquaint myself with the better philosophers,
Find where Socrates was martyred;—
No, I forgot,—there's a war going on there!
Yes; well, Hellenism must wait.

[*Looking at his watch.*]

It's ridiculous how long it takes
For the sun to rise. I haven't much time.
Well, from Troy—I had got as far as that—

[*He gets up and listens.*]

What in the world is that howling noise?

[*The sun rises.*]

STATUE OF MEMNON [*singing*].

> From the demi-God's ashes are rising
> The birds delighting.
> Zeus, All-surmising,
> Created them fighting.
> O wise owl, where
> Sleep my birds of the air?
> You must die or guess
> The song's mysteries.

PEER. No joking,—I'm sure a sound was made
By the statue! Music of the Past.
The stony voice was rising and falling.—
I'll write this down, for scholars to mull over.

[*He makes notes in his pocket-book.*]

'The statue sang. I distinctly heard it,
But didn't quite follow the sense of it.
The whole thing clearly hallucination:—
Nothing else of importance observed today.'

[*He goes on his way.*]

Sc. 12 ———————

[*Near the village of Gizeh. A great Sphinx carved out of the rocks.
In the distance Cairo's spires and minarets.
PEER GYNT enters. He looks attentively at the Sphinx, now
through his eyeglasses, now through his cupped hand.*]

PEER. Now, where in the world have I seen something
I dimly remember, like this monster?
For seen it I have, in the north or south.
A person? And if it was, then who?
It occurred to me afterwards that Memnon
Was like the so-called ancients of Dovre,
The way he sat there, as stiff as a ramrod,
With his bottom planted on stumps of pillars.—
But this fantastic mongrel creature,
This changeling, half lion and half a woman,—
Is he out of some legend, as well?

Or does he belong to some actual memory?
A legend! Now I remember the fellow!
Of course, it's the Boyg whose skull I thumped,—
I mean, dreamed I did—in a high fever.—

[*He moves closer.*]

The self-same eyes, and the same lips;—
Not quite so ponderous; rather more wily;
But, in every other way, identical.—
So that's it, Boyg; you look like a lion
When you're seen from behind, and in the daylight!
Do you still know riddles? Suppose we try.
Let's see if you answer the way you did last time.

[*Calling to the Sphinx.*]

Hi, Boyg, who are you?

VOICE [*behind the Sphinx*].   Ach, Sphinx, wer bist du?

PEER. What! Echo answers in German! Astonishing!

VOICE. Wer bist du?

PEER.   Speaks the language fluently!
That's a new observation; my own entirely.

[*He makes a note in his book.*]

'Echo in German. The Berlin dialect.'

[BEGRIFFENFELDT *comes from behind the Sphinx.*]

BEGRIFFENFELDT. A human being!

PEER.   Oh, so that's who was talking.

[*Makes another note.*]

'Arrived at a different conclusion later.'

BEGRIFFENFELDT [*gesticulating excitedly*].
Mein Herr, excuse me—! Eine Lebensfrage—!
What brought you here on this day of all days?

PEER. A visit. To greet a boyhood friend.

BEGRIFFENFELDT. Really? The Sphinx—?

PEER [*nodding*].   I used to know him.

BEGRIFFENFELDT. Staggering!—And after such a night!
  My forehead is pounding as though it would burst!
  You really know him? Tell me! Answer me!
  Can you say what he is?

PEER.   What he is? Quite easily.
  He is himself.

BEGRIFFENFELDT [*with a leap*]. Ha, the answer to the riddle of life
  Flashed across my eyes like lightning!
  You're absolutely sure he's himself?

PEER. Well, that's what he says, at any rate.

BEGRIFFENFELDT. Himself. Revolution is at hand!

[*He takes off his hat.*]

  May I know your name?

PEER.   I was christened Peer Gynt.

BEGRIFFENFELDT [*in quiet admiration*].
  Peer Gynt! An allegory! I might have guessed.—
  Peer Gynt? Which means, of course, the Unknown,
  The arrival, whose coming was foretold me—

PEER. Is that so? You mean you came here to meet—?

BEGRIFFENFELDT. Peer Gynt! Profound! Mysterious! Penetrating!
  Each word is a fathomless pit of knowledge!
  What are you?

PEER [*modestly*].   I've always attempted to be
  Myself. For the rest, you can see my passport.

BEGRIFFENFELDT. Again, you see, that mysterious word!

[*Grasping his wrists.*]

  To Cairo! Revelation's Emperor is found!

PEER. Emperor?

BEGRIFFENFELDT. Come!

PEER.   Am I really known—?

BEGRIFFENFELDT [*dragging* PEER *along with him*].
Revelation's Emperor—enthroned on Self!

Sc. 13 ——————

[*In Cairo. A large courtyard surrounded by high walls and buildings.
Barred windows; iron cages.*
THREE KEEPERS *in the courtyard.* A FOURTH *enters.*]

NEWCOMER. Schafmann; have you seen the director?

A KEEPER. He drove out long before it was light.

1ST KEEPER. I think he has been upset by something,
Because last night—

ANOTHER.   Sh! Be quiet;
He's here at the door!

[BEGRIFFENFELDT *leads* PEER GYNT *in, locks the gate and puts the key in
his pocket.*]

PEER [*to himself*].   He really is
A wonderfully gifted man; almost
All he says is incomprehensible.

[*He looks round him.*]

So this, then, is the Scholars' Club?

BEGRIFFENFELDT. Yes, you'll find the whole lot of them here;—
The Circle of the Seventy Commentators;
Recently increased by a hundred and sixty—

[*Calling to the* KEEPERS.]

Mickel, Schlingelberg, Schafmann, Fuchs,—
Get into the cages; hurry, now!

KEEPERS. We?

BEGRIFFENFELDT. Who else? Come along, come along!
It's a twizzling world; we must twizzle with it!
        SPINNING
[*Forcing them into the cages.*]

He arrived this morning, the mighty Peer;—
You must join the rest;—I needn't say more.

[*He locks the cage and throws the key into a well.*]

PEER. But, my dear Herr Doctor and Director—?

BEGRIFFENFELDT. Neither one nor the other! I used to be.—
Herr Peer, can you keep a secret?
There's something I want to get off my mind—

PEER [*increasingly uneasy*]. What is it?

BEGRIFFENFELDT.   Promise me not to tremble.

PEER. I'll do my best—

BEGRIFFENFELDT [*drawing him into a corner and whispering*].
                    Absolute Reason
Dropped dead last night at eleven o'clock.

PEER. God save us—!

BEGRIFFENFELDT.   Yes, it's most deplorable.
And in my position, as you can imagine,
Doubly unfortunate; because
Up to now this institution
Has been what is called a mad-house.

PEER.   A mad-house!

BEGRIFFENFELDT. Not now, you understand!

PEER [*pale, quietly*].   I realize
At last what this place is! And the man
Is a lunatic;—and no one knows it!

[*He tries to move away.*]

BEGRIFFENFELDT [*following him*].
I hope you have followed my meaning so far?
When I say 'dropped dead' I'm talking nonsense.
He's beside himself. Jumped out of his skin,—
Like my compatriot Münchhausen's fox.

PEER. Excuse me a moment—

BEGRIFFENFELDT [*holding on to him*]. I mean like an eel;—
  Not like a fox. Impaled through his eye;—
  He writhed on the wall—

PEER.   How can I save myself?

BEGRIFFENFELDT. A nick in the neck, and off comes his skin!

PEER. Demented! Utterly off his head!

BEGRIFFENFELDT. Now it's evident, and can't be kept hidden,—
  This *Von-Sich-Gehen* must result
  In complete revolution on land and sea.
  The individuals once called mad
  In fact became normal last night at eleven,
  To conform with the new conditions of Reason.
  And, if you look deeply into the matter,
  It's apparent that at the aforesaid time
  The so-called intelligent started to rave.

PEER. Talking of time, my time is limited—

BEGRIFFENFELDT. Your time? You've reminded me of something!

            [*He opens a door and calls.*]

  Come out! The future has been revealed!
  Reason is dead. Long live Peer Gynt!

PEER. No, my dear chap—!

            [*The LUNATICS gather one by one in the courtyard.*]

BEGRIFFENFELDT.   Come and pay your respects;
  Greet the rosy dawn of deliverance—
  Your Emperor is here!

PEER.   Their Emperor?

BEGRIFFENFELDT. Certainly!

PEER.   This is too great an honour,
  Far too much—

BEGRIFFENFELDT.   Don't let false modesty
  Affect you at a time like this.

PEER. But let me consider! No, I'm not the answer;
  You've stupefied me!

BEGRIFFENFELDT.   What, a man
  Who has solved the mystery of the Sphinx?
  Who is Himself?

PEER.   That's just the trouble.
  I am myself, in every respect.
  But here, if I understand, it's all
  A matter of being beside yourself.

BEGRIFFENFELDT. You're making a curious mistake.
  Here, a man's himself with a vengeance;
  Himself, and nothing else whatsoever;—
  The self full sail, full speed ahead.
  Each one shut up in the cask of self,
  Immersed in a fermentation of self,
  Hermetically sealed with the bung of self,
  The barrel pickled in a bath of self.
  No one has tears for other men's pain;
  No one accepts other men's notions.
  We're ourselves here, thought, word and deed,
  Ourselves right to the edge of the diving-board,—
  And so, now we come to elect an Emperor,
  You are obviously the perfect man.

PEER. Devil take it—!

BEGRIFFENFELDT.   Now don't be downhearted;
  Most things on earth are new to begin with.
  'One's self';—come; let me give an example;
  I'll pick one out at random for you—

                  [*To a gloomy figure.*]

  Good day, Huhu! Well, my lad,
  Still walking around looking miserable?

HUHU. What else can I do when generations
  Of people die one after another
  Without having themselves explained?

                  [*To* PEER GYNT.]

You're new in this place; would you like to hear?

PEER [*bowing*]. By all means!

HUHU.   Lend an ear, then.—
  In the East, the Malabaric beaches
  Clasp the sea like a golden girdle.
  Portuguese and Dutchmen grip
  The countryside with their own culture.
  Swarms of genuine Malabaris
  Live there, too. And so the language
  Got itself in a hopeless muddle;—
  Now they're in control of the country,
  But at one time, long ago,
  The ruler was the orangoutang.
  He was the master of the forest,
  Free to flail around and snarl
  Just as the hand of nature made him;
  He could bare his teeth and gawp
  And scream away to his heart's content,
  Top dog in his own kingdom.—
  Alas, then the foreign invaders
  Ruined the old language of the jungle.
  Four hundred years of unbroken night
  Brooded over the monkey world;
  And, as we know, a night of that length
  Leaves its mark on a population.—
  The ancient forest voice is silent;
  Not so much as a growl is heard there;—
  But if we want to express our thoughts
  We have to have speech to help us do it.
  No one can avoid the problem.
  The Dutchmen or the Portuguese,
  Mixed races like the Malabari,
  They're all of them in the same boat.—
  I've been trying to fight a battle
  For our authentic forest lingo,
  To reinvigorate the corpse,—
  Asserting the people's right to shriek,—
  Shrieked myself, to urge the need
  For shrieking in folk-literature.—

And small thanks I've had for it.—
Perhaps now you can understand
My worry. Thanks for listening;—
If you've any advice I'd welcome it!

PEER [*to himself*]. The saying is: when wolves are about
It's best to howl. [*Aloud.*]
            As I remember
Dear friend, in the Moroccan scrub
There's a tribe of orangoutangs
Who do without any spokesmen or poets;
Their language decidedly Malabarish!—
Charming and unimpeachable,—
Now if you, like other notables,
Went overseas, for the good of your country—

HUHU. Thanks, for paying such close attention;—
I'll do exactly as you say.—

[*With an expansive gesture.*]

The East has dispossessed its poets.
The West still has its orangoutangs! [*He goes.*]

BEGRIFFENFELDT. Now, was he himself? I should say he was.
Full of himself, not another thing,
Himself in every syllable,—
Himself because he's beside himself.
Come here! I'll show you another one,
Who since last night is equally rational.

[*To a* FELLAH *with a mummy on his back.*]

King Apis, how are you doing, your highness?

FELLAH [*to* PEER]. *Am* I King Apis?

PEER [*getting behind the doctor*]. I regret to say
I haven't quite grasped the situation;
But, from your manner, I can well believe it—

FELLAH. You are lying, as well.

BEGRIFFENFELDT.   Your royal highness
Should tell us just how the matter stands.

FELLAH. I'll tell you, then.

[*To* PEER GYNT.] Do you observe
Who it is I'm carrying on my back?
He used to be called King Apis; now
He goes under the name of mummy;
What's more, he is altogether dead.
He erected all the pyramids,
And hewed out the Great Sphinx,
And fought, as the doctor would say,
Rechts and *links* against the Turk.
Because of that the whole of Egypt
Has adored him as a god,
And set him up in all the temples
In the likeness of a bull.

But *I'm* King Apis; that's as clear
As daylight to me. If you can't
Understand me yet, you will.
You see, one day when King Apis
Was out hunting he dismounted
And went off by himself for a while,
On to my great-grandfather's land.

But the field that King Apis dunged
Yielded the corn I was nourished on;
And, if you want any further proof,
I can tell you I've got invisible horns.
Don't you think it's iniquitous
That nobody recognizes my power?
By birth I am Apis, of the land of Egypt,
But people think I'm only a peasant.—
Tell me what I should do; give me
Your honest advice;—the problem is how
To become more like King Apis the Great.

PEER. Your highness will have to build pyramids,
And carve an even greater Sphinx,
And fight, as the doctor would say,
Recht and *links* against the Turk.

FELLAH. Oh, yes, it's all very well to talk!
A peasant! A poor starving louse!
I've enough to do keeping my hut

Clear of rats and mice.—Quick, man,—
Think of something better than that,
A way to make me great and secure;—
And, what's more, identical
With King Apis here on my back!

PEER. Suppose your highness should hang yourself,
And then, in the bosom of the earth
Within the coffin's natural frontiers,
Remain immaculately dead?

FELLAH. So I will! My life for a halter!
Off to the gallows with flesh and blood!—
At first it will seem rather different,
But time will soon take care of that.

[*He goes to prepare to hang himself.*]

BEGRIFFENFELDT. There's a personality for you,—
A man of method—

PEER.   Yes, yes; I see;—
But he really means to hang himself!
God save us! I shall be sick;—
My thoughts are out of control!

BEGRIFFENFELDT.   A question
Of readjustment; it won't last long.

PEER. Readjustment? To what? Excuse me,—
I have to leave here—

BEGRIFFENFELDT [*restraining him*]. Are you mad?

PEER. Not yet—. Mad? Heaven forbid!

[*Uproar.* HUSSEIN, *a political minister, forces his way through the crowd.*]

HUSSEIN. I've been told an Emperor came here today.

[*To* PEER.]

Is it you?

PEER [*desperately*]. Yes, it's all been decided!

HUSSEIN. Good.—You have communications
  Needing an answer?

PEER [*tearing his hair*]. Come on! That's right;—
  The worse, the better!

HUSSEIN.   Will you do me
  The honour of dipping me in the ink?

                              [*Bowing deeply.*]

  I am a pen.

PEER [*bowing still lower*]. And I am simply
  A crumpled sheet of imperial parchment.

HUSSEIN. My history, sire, is briefly this:
  They think I'm a sand-box; I'm really a pen.

PEER. And mine, Mr. Pen, is very soon told:
  I'm a piece of paper no one has written on.

HUSSEIN. Men haven't an inkling of what I am for;
  They all want to use me for sprinkling sand!

PEER. When a woman owned me I was a book
  With a silver clasp. Mad or sane
  It's the same typographical error!

HUSSEIN. Imagine the frustration! To be a pen
  And never feel the edge of a penknife.

PEER [*leaping high*]. Imagine: to be a buck, who leaps
  From high in the air; comes plunging down,—
  And never feels the ground under him!

HUSSEIN. A knife! I'm blunt;—cut me and slit me!
  The world will be ruined if I'm not sharpened!

PEER. It's a pity the world, like all home-made things,
  Was thought by God to be very good.

BEGRIFFENFELDT. Here's a knife!

HUSSEIN [*grabbing it*].   Ah, how I shall lap the ink!
  What an ecstasy to slit oneself.

                              [*He cuts his throat.*]

BEGRIFFENFELDT [*moves to one side*]. Try not to spatter!

PEER [*in rising panic*].   Get hold of him!

HUSSEIN. Get hold of me! Yes, that's the word!
  Hold! Hold the pen! To a sheet of paper—!

[*He falls.*]

I'm worn out. Don't forget the postscript:
He lived and died a guided pen.

PEER [*fainting*]. What shall I—? What am I? O God—hold on!
  I'm whatever you want,—a Turk, a sinner,—
  A troll—; but help me; something has burst—!

[*He shrieks.*]

I can't for the moment think of your name;—
Help me, you—guardian of all madmen!

[*He sinks down unconscious.*]

BEGRIFFENFELDT [*with a wreath of straw in his hand, leaping astride him*].
  Now he's exalted into the mud;—
  He's beside himself—! His crowning moment!

[*He presses the wreath down on to* PEER GYNT's *head and shouts.*]

Long life! Long live the Emperor Self!

SCHAFMANN [*in the cage*]. Es lebe hoch der grosse Peer!

ACT FIVE

On board a ship in the North Sea off the Norwegian coast. Sunset. Stormy weather.

PEER GYNT, a vigorous old man with ice-grey hair and beard, is standing on the poop. He is dressed partly as a seaman, in a pea-jacket and high boots. His clothes are the worse for wear; he himself is weather-beaten and his expression harder. The CAPTAIN is standing beside the HELMSMAN at the wheel. The CREW is for'ard.

PEER [*leaning on the rail gazing towards the land*].
There's the Hallingskarv in its winter coat,
Parading itself in the evening sunlight.
And his brother Joekel leaning beside him,
Still with his green ice-jacket on.
And the Folgefonn: how superb she is,
Like a virgin asleep under snow-white linen.
Don't try any monkey-tricks, old men!
Stand still; remember you're made of granite.

CAPTAIN [*shouting for'ard*].
Two hands to the wheel—and loft the lantern!

PEER. It's blowing up rough.

CAPTAIN.   We're in for a storm.

PEER. Can you see the peaks of the Ronde from here?

CAPTAIN. Not a chance. They're away behind the snowfields.

PEER. Or the Blaahoy?

CAPTAIN.   No; but you can see
The peaks of Galdhoy from the rigging
On a clear day.

PEER.   Where's Haarteigen?

CAPTAIN [*pointing*]. Somewhere thereabouts.

PEER.   Yes, I thought so.

CAPTAIN. You seem familiar with these parts.

PEER. We sailed this way when I went abroad,
The last you swallow comes back first.

[*He spits and gazes at the coast.*]

Deep in there, in the blue shadows,
Where the valley blackens, like a narrow trench—
And below, beside the open fiords—
Isn't that where the people are tucked away?

[*He looks at the* CAPTAIN.]

The houses are spread out thin in this country.

CAPTAIN. Yes, they're few and far between.

PEER. Shall we make land before daybreak?

CAPTAIN.   Could do,
If the night doesn't bring dirty weather.

PEER. Thick cloud in the west.

CAPTAIN.   So I see.

PEER. When I come to settle up what I owe you,
Don't let me forget—I have a mind,
As the saying is, to contribute something
For the good of the crew.

CAPTAIN.   Thanks!

PEER.   It can't
Be much. I made a mint, but lost it.
Fate and I were at loggerheads.
You know what I've got on board, and that's
The lot; the rest has gone to the devil.

CAPTAIN. It's more than enough to impress your family
When you get back home.

PEER.   I've got no family.
No one's waiting for the rich old rascal.—
But it saves an emotional scene at the quayside!

CAPTAIN. Here comes the storm.

PEER.   Now, do remember,
    If any of the crew are really hard up
    I won't take too close a look at the money.

CAPTAIN. That's kind. Most of them find things difficult;
    They've all got wives and kids at home.
    Their pay alone doesn't go very far;
    But if they came back with something extra
    It would be a reunion they'd never forget.

PEER. What did you say? Wives and kids?
    Are they married?

CAPTAIN.   Married? Yes, all of 'em.
    But the cook is the one most badly off;
    Black hunger is seldom out of his house.

PEER. Married? They've someone waiting at home
    With a warm welcome? Eh?

CAPTAIN.   Why, yes,
    In their simple way.

PEER.   At night, unexpected,
    What then?

CAPTAIN. Somehow the wife would manage
    Some special treat.

PEER.   And light a lamp?

CAPTAIN. Or two, maybe; and schnapps with the supper.

PEER. And sit there snugly? Warm by the fire?
    The children with them? The room full of chatter;
    All talking at once, for the joy of the meeting?

CAPTAIN. Very likely. And all the more so
    Because of the kind suggestion you made
    Of a little extra—

PEER [*thumping the gunnel*]. I'm damned if I do it!
    Do you think I'm mad? Do you really expect me

To fork out for other people's kids?
I've slaved enough to earn what I've got!
Nobody's waiting for old Peer Gynt.

CAPTAIN. Well, please yourself; it's your own money.

PEER. You're right! It's mine, and nobody else's.
As soon as we drop anchor I'll pay
My cabin passage from Panama.
Then a drink for the crew, and that's the lot.
If I give any more you can beat me up!

CAPTAIN. A receipt, not a thrashing, is what I shall owe you.
But excuse me; it's blowing up for a storm.

*[He goes across the deck. It is getting dark; lights are lit in the cabin. The
sea gets rougher. Fog and thick clouds.]*

PEER. To have a cartload of kids at home,
Happy to be expecting you;
The thoughts of others for company.
There's no one at all who thinks of me.
A lamp on the table? I'll put that out.
I shall think of a way. I'll make them drunk;
Not one of the bastards will get ashore sober.
They shall greet their wives and children plastered,
Cursing and hammering on the table,
Scaring the family out of their wits!
The wives will run screaming out of the house,
Clutching the brats—all the pleasure shattered!

[The ship gives a violent lurch. PEER GYNT *staggers and almost loses his
balance.]*

Well, that was a good heel-over. The sea
Couldn't work harder if it was paid to.
Still its old self in these northern waters,
Cross currents headstrong and raging as ever!

[He listens.]

What was that yelling?

LOOK-OUT *[for'ard].*   A wreck to leeward!

CAPTAIN [*amidships, giving orders*].
Helm hard to starboard! Bring her up to the wind!

HELMSMAN. Are there men on the wreck?

LOOK-OUT.   I can make out three.

PEER. Lower the boat—

CAPTAIN.   One wave would swamp it.

[*He goes for'ard.*]

PEER. Why think about that?
[*To some of the* CREW.]   If you're men, to the rescue!
What the hell does it matter if you get a soaking?

BO'SUN. It's impossible in a sea like this.

PEER. They're yelling again! Look, the wind has dropped—
Cook, will you risk it? Quick! I'll pay you—

COOK. Not if you gave me twenty pounds!

PEER. You dogs! Cowards! Don't you realize
They're men with wives and children at home
And waiting—

BO'SUN.   Well, patience is a virtue.

CAPTAIN. Keep clear of that sea!

HELMSMAN.   The wreck's gone under.

PEER. Suddenly, silence?

BO'SUN.   If, as you say,
They were married, the world has got three new widows.

[*The storm increases.* PEER GYNT *goes aft.*]

PEER. There's no faith left among men any more;
No Christianity, as it used to be.
They do little good, and pray even less,
And have no respect for the powers above.—
In weather like this the Almighty's dangerous.
Those brutes should look out, and understand

It's risky playing with elephants.
But they openly snap their fingers at him!
He can't blame *me*; I was standing ready
To make the sacrifice, money in hand.
But what's my reward? The saying is:
'A clear conscience makes an easy pillow.'
Well, that may be true when you're on dry land,
But it's not worth a pinch of snuff at sea
Where a decent man is just one of the mob.
At sea you can't ever be yourself;
You must toe the line with the rest of the ship.
If the hour has struck for the bos'un and cook
I suppose I shall sink with the whole boiling;
One's personal merits count for nothing,
No more than a sausage at pig-sticking time.—
I've made the mistake of being too gentle,
And what thanks have I got for my trouble?
If I were younger I'd change my tactics
And try throwing my weight about a bit.
There's still time! They'll hear in the parish
Peer has come home again in triumph!
I'll get back the farm, by hook or by crook,
Rebuild it into a shining palace.
But I won't let anyone come inside!
They can stand at the gate, twisting their caps,
And beg and pray: there's no charge for that;
But nobody gets a penny of mine.
Since fate has thrashed *me* until I howled
I'll look for someone to thrash in return—

STRANGE PASSENGER [*standing in the dark beside* PEER GYNT *and speaking in a friendly way*]. Good evening!

PEER.   Good evening. What—? Who are you?

PASSENGER. Your fellow passenger, at your service.

PEER. Oh? I thought I was the only one.

PASSENGER. A wrong supposition, now rectified.

PEER. It's odd I haven't seen you before.

PASSENGER. I never come up on deck in the daytime.

PEER. You're ill, perhaps? You're as white as a sheet.

PASSENGER. Thank you, no—I'm perfectly fit.

PEER. It's a hell of a storm.

PASSENGER.   Yes, what a blessing!

PEER. A blessing?

PASSENGER.   The waves are as high as a house.
  Doesn't it make your mouth water?
  Think of the ships that are going to be wrecked,
  And the number of bodies washed ashore!

PEER. Heaven forbid!

PASSENGER.   Have you ever seen
  A man strangled, or hanged—or drowned?

PEER. That's enough of that!

PASSENGER.   The corpses laugh.
  But the laughter is forced. The majority of them
  Have taken a bite out of their tongues.

PEER. Keep away from me!

PASSENGER.   Just one question!
  If we, for example, ran on the rocks
  And sank in the dark—

PEER.   Is the danger likely?

PASSENGER. I don't really know how to answer that.
  But suppose I should float, and you go to the bottom—

PEER. Absurd!

PASSENGER.   It's just a possibility.
  But when a man's on the edge of his grave
  He weakens, and starts dealing out presents—

PEER [putting his hand in his pocket].
  Ah, it's money you want!

PASSENGER.   No, it isn't;
But would you be so good as to make me
A gift of your esteemed cadaver?

PEER. Now you've gone too far!

PASSENGER.   Simply the corpse!
For scientific research—

PEER.   Go away!

PASSENGER. My dear sir, it would be to your own advantage!
I'll open you up to the light of day.
I'm mainly looking for the seat of dreams,
But I'll carefully probe every gusset of you.

PEER. Be off!

PASSENGER.   My dear chap—just a drowned body!

PEER. Blasphemer! You're encouraging the storm!
It's too bad! We've already got wind and rain
And a mountainous sea, every indication
That we're not likely to make old bones,
And you're doing your best to hurry it on!

PASSENGER. I see you're not in the mood for business,
But, as you know, time brings its changes.

                    [*With a friendly bow.*]

We shall meet when you're drowning, if not before.
I may find you then in a better humour.

                    [*He goes into the cabin.*]

PEER. Sinister fellows, these scientists!
Such Godless talk.

                    [*To the* BO'SUN *as he passes.*]

                    A word with you, friend:
That passenger? What lunatic is he?

BO'SUN. You're the only passenger that I know of.

PEER. Just me? This is going from bad to worse.

[*To a* SHIP'S BOY *coming out of the cabin.*]

Who just went down the companion-ladder?

BOY. The ship's dog, sir! [*He goes.*]

WATCH [*calling*].   Land close ahead!

PEER. My trunk! My cases! All baggage on deck!

BO'SUN. We've other things to attend to.

PEER.   Captain!
It was all nonsense, only a joke—
Of course I'm willing to help the cook.

CAPTAIN. The jib has gone.

HELMSMAN.   There goes the foresail!

BO'SUN [*shouting from for'ard*]. Breakers under the bow!

CAPTAIN.   She's smashing up!

[*The ship strikes. Noise and confusion.*]

[*Close to land among the rocks and breakers. The ship is sinking. A dinghy with two men in it can be dimly seen through the fog. A wave breaks over it and swamps it; it overturns; a scream is heard; then everything silent for a while. Shortly afterwards the boat appears floating bottom upwards.*
PEER GYNT *comes to the surface near the boat.*]

PEER. Help! Send out a boat! Help! I'm drowning!
Save me, good Lord—as the prayer-book has it!

[*He clings on to the keel of the boat.*]

COOK [*coming up on the other side*].
Ah, heavenly Father—for my children's sake,
Have mercy! Let me get back to land!

[*He clings to the keel.*]

PEER. Let go!

COOK.　　　Let go!

PEER.　　　　　　I'll fight!

COOK.　　　　　　　　　So will I!

PEER. I'll push you under with my feet!
Get off! It won't carry both of us!

COOK. I know that. Give up!

PEER.　　　　　　　You give up!

COOK.　　　　　　　　　　Oh, yes?

[*They fight; the* COOK'S *hand is damaged; he clings on with the other one.*]

PEER. Take that hand away!

COOK.　　　　　　Oh, kind sir, spare me!
Remember my little ones at home!

PEER. I need life more than you: I still
Haven't got any children.

COOK.　　　　　Let go! You've lived
Your time; I'm young!

PEER.　　　　　　Be quick and sink—
You're dragging us down.

COOK.　　　　　　Have mercy on me!
Let go in the name of God! You've no one
Who's going to miss you and grieve for you.

[*He screams and lets go.*]

I'm drowning!

PEER [*grabbing him*]. I'll hold you up by the hair—
Say the Lord's prayer!

COOK.　　　　　I can't remember—
Everything's going dark—

PEER.　　　　　　Repeat
The important bits!

COOK.　　　　　'Give us this day—'

PEER. Skip that, cook; you're going to get
As much as you can swallow.

COOK.   'Give us this day—'

PEER. The same old song! You're a cook all right.

[*The* COOK *slips from his grasp.*]

COOK [*singing*]. 'Give us this day our—'

[*He goes under.*]

PEER.   Amen, my boy!
You remained yourself to your last gasp.

[*He swings himself up on to the boat.*]

While there's any life there's hope.

PASSENGER [*catching hold of the boat*].
Good morning!

PEER.   Hell!

PASSENGER.   I heard the shouting.
It's amusing to come across you again.
Well? You see, my prediction was true!

PEER. Let go! There's hardly room for one!

PASSENGER. I'm swimming with my left leg—
Floating, with only my fingertips
Touching the hull. But about your corpse—

PEER. Shut up!

PASSENGER.   The rest is over and done with.

PEER. Keep quiet, will you?

PASSENGER.   Just as you like. [*Silence.*]

PEER. Well?

PASSENGER. I'm keeping quiet.

PEER.   You demon!
What do you mean to do, then?

PASSENGER.   Wait.

PEER [*tearing his hair*].
  I shall go mad! What are you?

PASSENGER [*nodding*].   Friendly.

PEER. What else? Tell me!

PASSENGER.   What do you think?
  Who else do you know like me?

PEER.   The devil!

PASSENGER [*quietly*]. Does he usually carry the lantern
  On life's way through the night of fear?

PEER. I'm catching on! When we get down to it
  You mean you're a messenger of light?

PASSENGER. Friend, have you even once in six months
  Felt the reality of dread?

PEER. When a man's in danger, naturally
  He's afraid; but your words have a twist to them—

PASSENGER. Yes. Have you even once in your life
  Known the victory fear can give you?

PEER [*looking at him*]. If you came to open a door for me
  It's a pity you didn't come a bit sooner.
  What's the sense in choosing a time
  When the sea is about to swallow us up?

PASSENGER. The victory would be greater, you think,
  If you sat in comfort beside the fire?

PEER. Maybe not, but your talk was ridiculous.
  What effect did you think it could have?

PASSENGER. Where I come from the comic style
  Is valued as highly as the pathetic.

PEER. There's a time for everything; what floats
  A publican, as the saying goes,
  Would scupper a bishop.

PASSENGER.   The multitude
  Whose dust sleeps in the grave, don't wear
  The tragic mask day in, day out.

PEER. Leave me, you nightmare! Disappear!
  I don't want to die! I must get to land!

PASSENGER. As for that, don't worry; a fellow doesn't
  Die in the middle of the fifth act.

[*He glides away.*]

PEER. So I got it out of him at last.
  What an unpleasant moralizer!

Sc. 3 ————

[*A churchyard in a high mountain parish. A funeral.* A PRIEST *and*
PARISHIONERS. *The last verse of a psalm is being sung.* PEER GYNT
passes on the road.]

PEER [*at the gate*]. Here's a man going the way of all flesh.
  Praise be to God it isn't me.

[*He enters the churchyard.*]

PRIEST [*speaking at the graveside*].
  And now, when the soul has gone its way to judgement,
  And the flesh reposes here like an empty pod,
  Now, dear friends, we have a word to say
  About this dead man's journeying on earth.
    He wasn't rich, or of great understanding;
  His voice was small, he had no manly bearing;
  He gave his opinions shyly, uncertainly;
  Was scarcely master in his own house.
  In church, he walked like someone who would ask
  Permission to sit there among the others.
    He came from the Gudbrands valley, as you know.
  When he settled here he was hardly more than a boy;
  And you all remember how, up to the last,
  He always kept his right hand in his pocket.
    This right hand in the pocket was the thing
  That impressed the man's image on one's mind;
  And also the uneasiness, the shy
  Reticence when he walked into the room.
    But though he preferred to go his quiet way,
  And though he seemed a stranger here among us,

You all know (though he tried hard to conceal it)
There were only four fingers on the hand he hid.—
    I remember, on a morning many years ago,
A meeting at Lunde to enrol recruits.
It was war-time. Everybody was discussing
The country's ordeal, and what lay ahead.
    I stood watching. Sitting behind the table
Was the Captain, the parish clerk and some N.C.O.s.
They took the measure of one boy after another,
Swore them in and took them for the army.
The room was full, and outside you could hear
The crowd of young men laughing in the yard.
    Then a name was shouted. Another lad came forward,
Looking as pale as the snow on a glacier.
They called him nearer; he approached the table;
A piece of rag was tied round his right hand.
He gasped, swallowed, groped about for words,
But couldn't speak, in spite of the Captain's order.
However, his cheeks burning, stammering still
And speaking very quickly, he managed at last
To mumble something about an accidental
Slip of a scythe that sheared his finger off.
    Silence fell on the room, as soon as he said it.
Men exchanged looks, and their lips tightened.
They all stoned the boy with silent stares.
He felt the hail-storm, but he didn't see it.
The Captain, an elderly, grey-haired man, stood up,
Spat, pointed a finger, and said Get out!
    And the boy went. Everyone drew aside
So that he had to run the gauntlet between them.
He got as far as the door, then took to his heels
Up and off, across the fields and hillside,
Scrambling on over the shale and rocks,
To where his home was, high on the mountainside.
    Six months later he came to live down here
With a mother, a newborn child, and his wife-to-be.
He leased a plot of ground way up on the hill
Where the derelict land joins the parish of Lom.
He married as soon as he could; put up a house;
Ploughed the stony ground, and made his way,

As the waving gold of the little fields bore witness.
At church he kept his right hand in his pocket,
But back at home no doubt those nine fingers
Did the work of other people's ten.—
    One spring a flood carried it all away.
Only their lives were spared. Everything lost,
He set to work to make another clearing,
And by the autumn smoke rose up again
From a hillside farm, this time better sheltered.
Sheltered? Yes, from flood; but not from glaciers.
Two years later it all lay under the snow.
    Yet not even an avalanche could crack his courage.
He dug, and cleared, and carted away the debris,
And before the next winter-snows came drifting
His little house was built for the third time.
    He had three sons, three fine vigorous boys;
They should go to school, but the school was a long way off.
They could only reach the end of the valley road
By going through a narrow, precipitous pass.
What did he do? The eldest looked after himself
As best he could, and where the track dropped steeply
This man roped him round to give him support;
The others he bore in his arms and on his back.
    He toiled like this, year after year, until
The sons were men. Time, you would have thought,
To get some return. Three prosperous gentlemen
In the New World have managed to forget
Their Norwegian father and those journeys to school.
    His horizon was narrow. Apart from the few
Who were nearest to him, nothing else existed.
The ringing words that rouse other men's hearts
Meant nothing to him, more than a tinkle of bells.
Mankind, the fatherland, the highest ambitions
Of men, were only misty figures to him.
    But he had humility, humility, this man;
And after that call-up day he always carried
The shame of the verdict, as surely as his cheeks
Carried the burn of shyness, and his four
Fingers hid in his pocket.—An offender
Against the laws of the land? Yes, indeed!

But there's one thing that shines above the law,
As truly as the bright tent of Glitretind
Has even higher peaks of cloud above it.
He was a poor patriot. To State
And Church, an unproductive tree. But there
On the brow of the hill, within the narrow
Circle of family, where his work was done,
There he was great, because he was himself.
He matched up to the living sound he was born with.
His life was like a music on muted strings.

   So peace be with you, silent warrior,
Who strove and fell in the peasant's little war!
We won't try to probe the ways of his heart.
That's for his Maker, not for us, to do.
But I can hold this hope, with little doubt:
He is not maimed now as he stands before his God.

[*The* CONGREGATION *disperses and goes. Only* PEER GYNT *is left.*]

PEER. Now that's what I call Christianity!
Nothing unpleasant to jar the mind;
And the theme—to be your unshakeable self,
Which was central to his argument—
Was, on the whole, just as uplifting.

[*Looking down into the grave.*]

Was it he who hacked through his knuckle, I wonder,
That day I was chopping trees in the forest?
Who knows? If I wasn't standing here
With my stick by the grave of this kindred spirit,
I could believe it was I who slept
In a living dream, hearing my praises.—
It's a good and generous Christian habit
To throw a benevolent backward glance
Over the life of the departed.
I wouldn't at all mind being judged
By such an excellent parish priest.
Well, I dare say there's enough time left
Before the gravedigger asks me in;
Leave well alone, as the scriptures say;
And 'Cross your bridge when you come to it'—

And 'Don't pay for your funeral till you've had it'
The Church, after all, is the true consoler.
I didn't appreciate that before;
But now I can see how soothing it is
To be reassured, on the best authority,
That as you sow, so shall you reap.—
You must be yourself: look after yourself
And yours, in small things as well as great.
If luck goes against you, at least there's the comfort
That you lived according to the instructions.—
Now home! Though the road is steep and narrow
And Fate ironical to the last,
Old Peer Gynt will gang his own gait
And be what he is: poor but virtuous.

[*He goes.*]

Sc. 4 ————————

[*A hillside with a dried river-bed. A mill in ruins beside the river;
the ground torn up; desolation all around. Higher up a large farmhouse. An auction is going on in front of the house. A large
crowd, drinking noisily.*

    PEER GYNT *is sitting on a heap of stones by the mill.*]

PEER. Forward or back, it's the same distance;
    Out or in, it's equally narrow.
    Time consumes, and rivers erode.
    Go round and about, said the Boyg.—You have to
    Here!

A MAN IN MOURNING. Now only the rubbish is left.

[*He sees* PEER GYNT.]

    Strangers, as well? God bless you, friend.

PEER. Well met. This place is lively today.
    Is it a christening or a wedding?

MAN IN MOURNING. Better to call it a house-warming.
    The bride is lying in a bed of worms.

PEER. And the worms are fighting over what's left.

MAN IN MOURNING. It's all finished now. The end of the song.

PEER. All songs wind up in the same way;
And I sang them all when I was a boy.

A TWENTY-YEAR-OLD [*with a casting ladle*].
Here, look at the fine thing I've bought!
Peer Gynt made silver buttons in this.

ANOTHER. How about this? A ha'penny for the money-bag!

A THIRD. That all? The pedlar's pack was tuppence!

PEER. Peer Gynt? Who was *he*?

MAN IN MOURNING.   He was part of the life
Of the dead woman and Aslak the smith.

A MAN IN GREY. You're forgetting me! Are you drunk and stupid?

MAN IN MOURNING. You're forgetting the door of the storehouse at
Haegstad!

MAN IN GREY. That's true; but you've never been very particular.

MAN IN MOURNING. As long as she don't make a fool out of Death—

MAN IN GREY. Come on, brother! Let's drink to our fellowship!

MAN IN MOURNING. Fellowship be damned. You're pissed already.

MAN IN GREY. Nonsense. Blood's not so thin we don't
Know we're all a part of Peer Gynt.

[*Takes him off with him.*]

PEER [*to himself*]. I seem to have come on some old acquaintances.

A BOY [*calling after the* MAN IN MOURNING].
Your poor old mother will be after you, Aslak,
If you drink too much!

PEER [*getting up*].   That old country saying
Doesn't hold good in this neighbourhood:
'The deeper you dig the better the smell.'

A BOY [*with a bear skin*].
Look, the Cat of Dovre! Well, only the skin.
The one that chased the trolls away
On Christmas Eve.

ANOTHER [*with a reindeer skull*]. Here's the marvellous
    Buck that carried Peer Gynt on its back
    Along the razor-edge of the Gjendin.

A THIRD [*with a hammer, shouting at the* MAN IN MOURNING].
    Hey, Aslak, remember this sledge-hammer?
    Isn't it the one that you were using
    When the Devil flew up and split the ceiling?

FOURTH [*empty-handed*]. Matt Moen, here's the invisible cloak
    Peer Gynt and Ingrid flew through the air in.

PEER. Give me some brandy! I'm feeling old;
    I'll hold an auction of all my junk!

A BOY. What have you got to auction?

PEER.   A palace;
    Solidly built, up in the Ronde.

BOY. A button is bid!

PEER.   Why not make it a schnapps?
    A terrible shame to bid less than that.

ANOTHER. He's a humorist, this old man!

PEER [*shouts*].   My horse,
    Greycoat,—who bids?

ONE IN THE CROWD. Where is he?

PEER.   Away
    In the west by the sunset! He can gallop
    As fast—as fast as Peer Gynt could lie.

VOICES. What else is there?

PEER.   Gold and scrap metal!
    Bought with a shipwreck; I'll sell at a loss.

A BOY. Put it up!

PEER.   First lot: a dream
    About a book with a silver clasp.
    I'll let it go for a hook and eye.

BOY. To hell with dreams!

PEER.   Second lot: my Empire!
  I'll throw it to the crowd; you can scramble for it!

BOY. And the crown with it?

PEER.   Of lovely straw.
  It will fit the first man who puts it on.
  And here's still more! An addled egg!
  A madman's grey hair! A prophet's beard!
  All these to whoever shows me a signpost
  That says: This is the road to go!

BAILIFF [*who has come up*].
  The way you're behaving, my man, your road
  Is going to lead you straight to the lock-up.

PEER [*hat in hand*]. Most likely. But, tell me, who was Peer Gynt?

BAILIFF. Come off it—

PEER.   No, really, I want to know.

BAILIFF. An appalling story-teller, they say.

PEER. Story-teller?

BAILIFF.   Yes—he pretended
  He'd done every mighty thing in the book.
  But, excuse me, I've other things to do—

                    [*He goes.*]

PEER. And where is he now, this remarkable man?

OLDER MAN. He went overseas to a foreign land;
  And came off badly, as you might expect.
  A long time ago now he was hanged.

PEER. Hanged? Well, well! I thought as much;
  Poor Peer Gynt was himself to the last.

                    [*He bows.*]

Goodbye—and thanks for the pleasant day!

      [*He walks a few steps and stops again.*]

Well, boys and girls, by way of return
Would you like to hear a traveller's tale?

SEVERAL. Yes, can you tell one?

PEER.   Nothing can stop me.

[He comes nearer; a strange look comes over him.]

I was digging for gold in San Francisco.
The whole town was swarming with mountebanks.
One played the fiddle with his toes;
One danced a fandango on his knees;
Another, I heard, went on reciting
While a hole was being bored through his skull.
This motley lot were joined by the Devil,
To try his luck, like so many others.
His line was this: to be able to grunt
Convincingly like a real pig.
His personality drew the crowd
Even though they didn't know who he was.
The house was full; expectation high.
With a swirl of his cloak he took the stage;
Man muss sich drappieren, as the Germans say.
But under his cloak—nobody knew it—
He had managed to smuggle in a pig.
And now he started on his performance.
The Devil pinched, and the pig sang out.
It was all a kind of extravaganza
On porcine life, enslaved and free:
The finale a squeal, as the creature is butchered;
After which the performer bowed low and withdrew.—
The experts started appraising the act:
The artistic effect was condemned and praised;
Some found the vocal quality thin;
Others considered the death-shriek too studied;
But everybody agreed, *qua* grunt,
The performance was grossly overdone.—
So that's what he got for being a fool
And failing to gauge the taste of his public.

[He bows and leaves. An uncertain silence falls over the crowd.]

*[Whitsun Eve. Deep in the forest. A little way off, in a clearing,
a cottage with reindeer horns over the door.*

PEER GYNT *on his hands and knees looking for wild onions in the
undergrowth.]*

PEER. This is one stage of the journey. Where next?
Try everything, and then choose the best.
Which is what I've done—starting with Caesar,
And all down the scale to Nebuchadnezzar.
So I *couldn't* leave Biblical history out.
The old boy has had to run back to his mother.
'From earth art thou come', as they say in the scriptures.
The main purpose in life is filling the belly.
Fill it with onions? That isn't much good;
I shall have to be cunning and set some traps.
There's a stream of water, I shan't be thirsty,
And at least I rank first in the animal world.
And when I die—which I shall, most likely—
I'll crawl under a fallen tree,
Heap dead leaves over me, as a bear does,
And scratch on the tree-trunk in big letters:
Here lies Peer Gynt, that decent fellow,
Emperor of all the other animals.
Emperor? *[He laughs inwardly.]*
            You soothsaying jackass!
You're no Emperor; you're an onion.
Now I shall peel you, good old Peer!
It won't help, either, to cry for mercy.

[He takes the onion and peels off the layers.]

Off with the outer, tattered layer;
The shipwrecked man hanging on to the boat.
Here's the passenger, shabby and thin,
But the taste has a hint of the real Peer Gynt.
And, inside that, the gold-digging me;
The juice has gone—if it ever had any.
This coarse bit here, with the thick skin,
Is the fur-trapper from Hudson Bay.
The next bit looks like a crown; many thanks!
We'll throw that away without further comment.

Now the ancient-historian, brief but vigorous.
This one's the prophet, fresh and sappy,
Stinking of lies, as they say, enough
To make an honest man's eyes water.
This veil, which rolls so smoothly off,
Is the gentleman living in luxury.
The next seems sick. It's got black streaks:
The black represents either priest or nigger.

[*He pulls several layers off at once.*]

What a tremendous number of layers!
Will the heart of it never come to light?

[*He pulls the whole onion to pieces.*]

My God, no, it won't! Right to the centre
It's all made of layers—but smaller and smaller.
Nature is witty! [*He throws the rest away.*]
                    To hell with brooding!
Trudging round your thoughts you can come a cropper.
Well, that's not something that need worry me
Since I'm already down on all fours.

[*Scratching his neck.*]

A peculiar business, this whole affair!
Life, they say, has a card up its sleeve.
But it disappears when you try to take it,
And you've something else in your hand—or nothing.

[*He has come near to the hut, suddenly sees it and starts.*]

This hut? On the moor—! Ha! [*Rubs his eyes.*] It's just
As if I had known it before at some time.—
The reindeer horns branching over the door!
A mermaid, fish from the navel downwards!
Lies! There's no mermaid—Nails, planks,
And a lock to keep out hobgoblin thoughts . . .!

SOLVEIG [*singing inside*].
                    Now all is ready for Whitsun Eve,
                         Distant lover, dearest and best:
                              Will you come back soon?

Is the burden so very great?
Take time to rest.
I still shall wait
Here as I promised, under the moon.

PEER [*getting up, quiet and deathly pale*].
One has remembered—and one has forgotten.
One has squandered, and one has saved,
O truth! And time can't be redeemed!
O terror! Here's where my empire was!

[*He runs away down the forest path.*]

Sc. 6 ─────────────

[*Night. A heath; fir-trees. A forest fire has been raging; charred tree-trunks for miles around. White trails of mist here and there over the ground.*
PEER GYNT *runs across the heath.*]

PEER. Scuds of fog, dust in the wind,
And ashes—here's enough to build with!
Stench and decay at the centre of it:
All a whited sepulchre.
The pyramid is founded on
Fantasy, dreams, and still-born knowledge;
And over them the edifice
Goes up and up in steps of lies.
Truth scorned, repentance shunned,
Flaunt like a banner at the summit,
And sound the trump of doomsday with their
'Petrus Gyntus Caesar fecit!' [*He listens.*]
Why are children's voices weeping?
Weeping, and yet almost singing.—
And balls of yarn roll at my feet!

[*Kicking.*]

Get out of the road! You're in my way!

BALLS OF YARN [*on the ground*].
We are thoughts:
You should have thought us,

                          Taught us
                          How to use our legs!

PEER [*going round them*].
   I gave my life to one thought only—
   A botched-up job, with a crooked shinbone!

BALLS OF YARN.   We should have soared aloft
                        Like ringing voices—
                        Instead we have become
                        Grey balls of yarn.

PEER [*stumbling*]. Bundle! You damned underling!
   Trying to trip up your father, are you?

                          [*He runs from them.*]

WITHERED LEAVES [*flying before the wind*].
                          We are the password
                          You should have given!
                          Look how your lethargy
                          Stripped us to skeletons.
                          Worms have devoured us
                          Down to the veins;
                          We have never held fruit
                          In our cupped green hands.

PEER. But still, you haven't been born for nothing.
   Lie quiet on the ground, and make good compost.

A SIGHING IN THE AIR.
                          We are songs;
                          You should have sung us!
                          Thousands of times
                          You have stifled us.
                          We have been waiting
                          Under your heart,
                          But were never sent for.
                          Death to your voice!

PEER. And death to you, you ludicrous jingle!
   What time did I have for versifying?

                          [*He tries to take a short cut.*]

DEWDROPS [*dripping from the branches*].

> We are the tears
> You never let fall.
> We could have melted
> The skewering ice.
> But the point has gone
> Far into your breast,
> And the flesh closed up.
> We can do nothing now.

PEER. Thanks; I wept in the Ronde mountain,
And ended up with a tail of woe.

BROKEN STRAWS.

> We are the deeds
> That you left undone.
> Doubt, like a strangler,
> Choked and destroyed us.
> On Judgement Day
> We shall come crowding
> And tell all we know—
> You'll pay for it then!

PEER. Scoundrels! How dare you indict me
Because of things I *haven't* done?

[*He hurries away from them.*]

AASE'S VOICE [*far away*].

> Lord, what a reckless driver!
> Hey, you've tipped me over!
> There's snow on the ground, my boy.
> I'm smothered and rolled in flour.
> You brought me the wrong road.
> Eh, son? Where's the castle?
> The Devil has nousled you
> With that stick out of the cupboard!

PEER. The sooner I'm out of here the better.
If a chap has to carry the sins of the Devil
He wouldn't take long to be flat on the ground.
One's own weigh quite enough, without that.

[*He runs off.*]

Sc. 7

[*Another part of the heath.*]

PEER [*sings*]. Sexton! Sexton! What are you at?
             Sing of what lying under the sod is!
             A piece of crêpe round the brim of the hat—
             I've a host of dead, and follow their bodies!

[*The* BUTTONMOULDER, *with his box of tools and a large casting-ladle, comes from a side path.*]

BUTTONMOULDER. Well met, good old man!

PEER.   Good evening, friend!

BUTTONMOULDER. The man's in a hurry. Where is he off to?

PEER. To a wake.

BUTTONMOULDER. Indeed? I don't see very well;
  Excuse me, your name wouldn't be Peer?

PEER. Peer Gynt, as they say.

BUTTONMOULDER.   What a piece of luck!
  Peer Gynt is the man I was sent to find.

PEER. Really? What do you want?

BUTTONMOULDER.   I'll tell you.
  I'm a buttonmoulder. You have to go
  Into my ladle.

PEER.   Why into your ladle?

BUTTONMOULDER. To be melted down.

PEER.   Melted down?

BUTTONMOULDER. Here it is, well scoured and empty.
  Your grave is dug, your coffin reserved.
  The worms will luxuriate in your carcass,
  But my orders are to fetch your soul
  On my master's behalf, as soon as I can.

PEER. Impossible! Not like this, without warning!

BUTTONMOULDER. It's an old custom with births and deaths
  To choose the festive day in secret
  Without informing the guest of honour.

PEER. Yes, of course.—I'm a bit confused.
You are—?

BUTTONHOLDER. I told you: a buttonmoulder.

PEER. I understand! A favourite child
Has a lot of nicknames. Well, then, Peer:
So this is where you're ending up!
But it's grossly unfair treatment, old chap!
I know I deserve more consideration;
I'm not as bad as you seem to think;
I've done a great deal of good in the world.
At the very worst you can say I'm a bungler,
But certainly not an exceptional sinner.

BUTTONMOULDER. No, that's exactly the complication.
Not a sinner at all, in the deeper sense;
Which is why you're excused the pains of torment,
And arrive, like others, in the casting-ladle.

PEER. Call it what you like—ladle or limbo;
Mild or bitter, they're both still beer.
Get behind me, Satan!

BUTTONMOULDER.   Are you being so rude
As to think I trot round on a horse's hoof?

PEER. On a horse's hoof or a fox's claws—
Clear off; and be careful what you get up to!

BUTTONMOULDER. There seems to be some misapprehension.
We're both in a hurry, so, to save time,
I'll try and explain what it's all about.
You're not—as you yourself have said—
A sinner on any heroic scale;
Not really even mediocre—

PEER. Now you're talking sense.

BUTTONMOULDER.   Just wait a minute.
To call you good would be going too far—

PEER. I never laid claim to any such thing.

BUTTONMOULDER. Neither one nor the other, merely so-so.
  Sinners of really impressive stature
  Aren't to be met with nowadays.
  It takes more than paddling in the dirt;
  It takes strength and a serious mind to sin.

PEER. Yes, I agree with all you say;
  One must go full blast, like the old Berserks.

BUTTONMOULDER. But you, on the contrary, took sin lightly.

PEER. On the surface, friend, like a splash of mud.

BUTTONMOULDER. We begin to agree. Fire and brimstone
  Aren't the things for a mud-splashed man.

PEER. And, therefore, I can go as I came?

BUTTONMOULDER. No; therefore, friend, I must melt you down.

PEER. What sort of tricks have you been inventing
  Here at home, while I've been away?

BUTTONMOULDER. A technique as old as the serpent in Eden,
  For keeping up the standard of values.
  You've worked at the craft; you know how often
  A casting turns out to be—if I
  May put it plainly—no better than shit.
  Sometimes the buttons had no eyelets.
  So what did you do?

PEER.   Threw the trash away.

BUTTONMOULDER. That's right; Jon Gynt was famous for squandering
  While there was anything left in his purse.
  But the Master, you see, is a thrifty one,
  Which is why he's become so immensely well-off.
  He doesn't throw anything away
  Which he thinks he can use as raw material.
  You were meant to be a glinting button
  On the world's coat, but the eyelet split;
  So you have to go into the reject-box,
  And merge with the masses, as they say.

PEER. You're not really intending to melt me down
  With Tom, Dick and Harry into something different?

BUTTONMOULDER. Yes, that's precisely what I *am* intending.
    We've done it plenty of times before.
    At Kongsberg they do the same thing with coins
    Which have worn smooth in circulation.

PEER. But this is nothing but sordid cheese-paring!
    My very dear friend, you must let me off!
    A smooth coin, an imperfect button—
    What's that to a man in your Master's position?

BUTTONMOULDER. Ah, but since, and so far as, the spirit is in you,
    There's always the value you have as metal.

PEER. No, I say, no! I'll fight tooth and nail!
    Anything, anything rather than that!

BUTTONMOULDER. But what? Come now, have some commonsense.
    You're not light enough to go up to heaven.

PEER. I'm easily pleased; I don't aim high;
    But I won't give up a grain of my Self.
    Put me on trial, as it's always done!
    Let me serve a term with him of the hoof—
    For a hundred years, if it has to be;
    I dare say that could be endured
    As it's only a matter of moral torment
    And therefore can't be so monumental.
    It's a metamorphosis, as the fox said
    When it was skinned; one waits; the hour
    Of deliverance comes; you fill in time,
    And look forward meanwhile to better days.
    But this other idea—to be absorbed
    Like a molecule into a foreign body—
    This ladle affair, this Gynt destruction,
    Rouses my innermost soul to revolt!

BUTTONMOULDER. But, my dear Peer, you needn't get
    So worked up over such a minor matter.
    Up to now you've never been yourself;
    What difference does it make if you vanish completely?

PEER. I've never been—? I could almost laugh!
    Peer Gynt has been something else, is that it?

No, buttonmoulder, you judge without seeing.
If you could scrutinize my vitals
You would find Peer there, and only Peer,
And nothing but Peer, neither more nor less.

BUTTONMOULDER. That isn't possible. Here are my orders.
You can see for yourself: Collect Peer Gynt.
He defied the purpose of his life.
Put him in the ladle as damaged goods.

PEER. What nonsense! They must have got the name wrong.
Does it really say Peer? Not Rasmus or Jon?

BUTTONMOULDER. They were melted down a long while ago.
Come quietly, and don't waste any more time!

PEER. I'm damned if I will! A pretty thing
If tomorrow you found it meant somebody else.
You ought to be jolly careful, my man!
Remember what you'll be accountable for—

BUTTONMOULDER. I have it in writing—

PEER.   At least give me time!

BUTTONMOULDER. What good will it do you?

PEER.   I'll prove to you
That I was myself all through my life;
Isn't that what we're arguing over?

BUTTONMOULDER. Prove? What with?

PEER.   With witnesses
And testimonials.

BUTTONMOULDER. I'm sorry,
But I think the Master will turn them down.

PEER. Impossible! Well, we won't cross our bridges.
Dear man, let me borrow myself for a bit.
I won't be long. You're born only once,
And you like to hang on to the self you began with.
Well, is it agreed?

BUTTONMOULDER.   All right, so be it.
But we'll meet at the next cross-road, remember.

[PEER GYNT *runs off.*]

Sc.8 ─────────────

[*Further on across the heath.* PEER GYNT *enters at full speed.*]

PEER. Time is money, as the saying goes.
I wish I knew where that cross-road is—
It might be near, or a long way yet.
The earth's as hot as a branding iron.
A witness! A witness! Where can I find them?
It's almost unthinkable here in the forest.
The world's a mess! What a state of affairs
When a man has to prove his obvious right!

[*A* CROOKED OLD MAN, *with a stick in his hand and a bag over his shoulder, trudges up to him.*]

OLD MAN [*stopping*]. A copper for a poor beggar, dear sir!

PEER. Sorry; I've no small change at the moment.

OLD MAN. Prince Peer! Surely not? Fancy us meeting!

PEER. Who are *you*?

OLD MAN.   Do you mean you don't remember
The old man in the Ronde?

PEER.   You're not—?

OLD MAN. The Master of Dovre.

PEER.   The Master of Dovre?
Really? The Master of Dovre? You swear it?

DOVRE-MASTER. Alas, I've come down in the world since then.

PEER. Done for?

DOVRE-MASTER. Stripped of all I possessed.
I'm plodding the roads, like a starving wolf.

PEER. Hurrah! A witness as useful as you
Doesn't grow on trees!

L

DOVRE-MASTER.   Your highness the prince
Has gone grey, too, since we last met.

PEER. My dear father-in-law, the years are locusts.
Well, we won't think of our private affairs—
Particularly about family quarrels.
I was a madman in those days—

DOVRE-MASTER.   Yes,
The prince was young. And what don't we do then?
But the prince was wise to turn down his bride;
It saved him a lot of shame and resentment.
Since then, I'm afraid, she has gone to the dogs.

PEER. Is that so?

DOVRE-MASTER. The world turned its back on her.
And, imagine, she's living now with Trond.

PEER. Which Trond?

DOVRE-MASTER.   The Val-mountain Trond.

PEER.   With him?
The one I stole the goat-girls away from!

DOVRE-MASTER. But my grandson's turned into a strapping fellow,
With bouncing children all over the country.

PEER. Well, save all that for some other time;
Something quite different is troubling me.—
I find myself in a tricky position,
And need someone to give me a character.
Help me in this, father-in-law.
And I'll scrape up the price of a drink for you.

DOVRE-MASTER. Can I really be useful to the prince?
Will you give me a reference in return?

PEER. Gladly. I'm rather short of cash,
Have to economize all ways up.
But let me explain what's wrong. You remember
The night I asked for your daughter's hand?

DOVRE-MASTER. Of course, my prince!

PEER.   Stop calling me prince!
  Anyhow, you wanted by sheer brute force
  To distort my vision with a slit in the eye,
  And change me from Peer Gynt into a troll.
  What did I do? I stood out against it,
  Swore I would stand on my own two feet;
  I sacrificed love and power and glory
  For the sake of remaining my own true self.
  This is what you must swear to in court.—

DOVRE-MASTER. But I can't!

PEER.   What are you talking about?

DOVRE-MASTER. Is he going to force me to tell a lie?
  He surely remembers he put on troll breeches,
  And tasted the mead—?

PEER.   You pushed me that far,
  But I flatly refused the final test.
  And that's how you know what a man is worth.
  It's the ultimate verse that makes the point.

DOVRE-MASTER. But the end of it, Peer, was quite the opposite.

PEER. What do you mean?

DOVRE-MASTER.   When you left the Ronde
  You wrote on your heart my favourite maxim.

PEER. What maxim?

DOVRE-MASTER.   The potent, thundering Word.

PEER. The Word?

DOVRE-MASTER.   Which separates mankind
  From trolls: to yourself be all-sufficient!

PEER [*recoiling a step*]. Sufficient!

DOVRE-MASTER.   And for all you're worth
  You've been living up to it ever since.

PEER. I? Peer Gynt?

DOVRE-MASTER [*weeping*]. What ingratitude!
  You've lived as a troll without admitting it.

The word I taught you gave you the power
To hoist yourself up to the top of the ladder;
And then you come here and turn up your nose
At me and the word you owe it all to.

PEER. Sufficient! A mountain troll! An egoist!
This must be nonsense, I'm perfectly certain!

DOVRE-MASTER [*pulling out a bundle of old newspapers*].
I suppose you think we haven't got newspapers?
Wait: I can show you in black and red
How the *Bloksberg Post* applauds and reveres you;
As the *Hekle Mountain Times* has done
Ever since the winter you left the country.—
Would you care to read them? You're very welcome.
Here's an article signed 'Stallionhoof'.
And look at this: 'On Troll Nationalism'.
The writer makes a point of the fact
That horns and tails are of small importance
As long as a good skin-grafting is there.
'Our sufficiency', he concludes, 'gives a man
The hall-mark of the troll', and then
He goes on to quote *you* as a fine example.

PEER. A mountain troll? I?

DOVRE-MASTER.   Of course.

PEER. As if I had never gone away?
Could have sat in the Ronde in peace and comfort?
Saved all that trouble and effort and shoe-leather?
Peer Gynt—a troll? It's absurd! Goodbye!
Here's something to buy yourself some tobacco.

DOVRE-MASTER. No, kind Prince Peer!

PEER.   Let me go! You're mad
Or in your dotage. Find a hospital!

DOVRE-MASTER. Ah, that's just what I'm on the look-out for.
But my grandson's offspring, as I said before,
Have made themselves such a power in the land;
And they say I only exist in books.
It's said: One's kin are less than kind.

Poor me, I've learnt the truth of that.
It's a terrible life, being a legend!

PEER. Dear man, you're not the only one
To suffer from that.

DOVRE-MASTER. And we haven't even
A pension fund, a savings bank
Or a poor box. In the Ronde, of course,
Such things would be unthinkable.

PEER. Their damned 'Sufficient' was all that mattered.

DOVRE-MASTER. The Prince can't complain about that word,
Or if, in some way or other, he could—

PEER. Look, you've got things completely wrong;
I'm on my beam ends myself, as they say.

DOVRE-MASTER. Is that possible? The prince a pauper?

PEER. Totally. My royal ego's in hock.
And it's all your fault, you bloody trolls!
That's what comes of keeping bad company.

DOVRE-MASTER. So my hopes have come unstuck again!
Farewell! It's best I make for the town.—

PEER. What will you do there?

DOVRE-MASTER. Go on the stage.
They've been advertising for national types.

PEER. The best of luck; remember me to them.
If I can get free I'll follow your lead.
I'll write a farce of crazy profundity
And call it 'Sic transit gloria mundi'.

[*He runs off down the path; the* DOVRE-MASTER *calls after him.*]

Sc. 9 ————

[*At a cross-road.*]

PEER. Now all is at stake as never before!
The trollish word has sealed my fate.

The ship's gone down; I must cling to the flotsam.
Anything, except the rubbish heap.

BUTTONMOULDER [*at the cross-road*].
Well, have you got your recommendation?

PEER. Have we come to the cross-road? That's quick work!

BUTTONMOULDER. I can see on your face, like a public announcement,
What the note says, before I've read it.

PEER. I was tired of searching; I might have got lost—

BUTTONMOULDER. Yes; and where in the world does it lead you?

PEER. Where, indeed! In the forest, with night coming on.

BUTTONMOULDER. But here's an old tramp. Shall we ask him over?

PEER. No, let him go. He's drunk, my dear man!

BUTTONMOULDER. But he might be able—

PEER.   Ssh! No—ignore him.

BUTTONMOULDER. Well, shall we begin?

PEER.   There's just one question.
What, exactly, is 'being one's self'?

BUTTONMOULDER. A curious question, especially
From a man who not very long ago—

PEER. Give me a short, straightforward answer.

BUTTONMOULDER. To be one's self is to kill one's self.
I doubt if that answer means anything to you.
So we'll put it this way: to show unmistakably
The Master's intention whatever you're doing.

PEER. But what if a man has never discovered
What the Master intended?

BUTTONMOULDER.   Then he must sense it.

PEER. But such guesses are often wide of the mark,
And one goes *ad undas* in mid-career.

BUTTONMOULDER. Exactly, Peer Gynt; incomprehension
Gives the Devil his best catch.

PEER. It seems incredibly complicated.—
    Look here, I'll give up being myself—
    I can see it's not going to be easy to prove.
    I accept that part of my cause as lost.
    But just now, wandering alone on the moor,
    I felt the shoes of my conscience pinching;
    I said to myself: after all, you're a sinner—

BUTTONMOULDER. Now you're taking us back to where we began.

PEER. Not quite; I mean a tremendous sinner;
    Not only in deed, in word and intention.
    Abroad I lived one hell of a life—

BUTTONMOULDER. No doubt; may I see the testimonial?

PEER. All right; don't rush me. I'll find a priest,
    Make a quick confession, and bring back his verdict.

BUTTONMOULDER. Yes, if you do that you obviously
    Needn't end up in the casting-ladle.
    But my orders, Peer—

PEER.   That paper's old;
    It clearly dates back to ages ago
    When I slopped around like a good-for-nothing,
    Playing the prophet and trusting in Fate.
    Well, may I try?

BUTTONMOULDER. But—!

PEER.   Dear, good friend,
    I'm sure you haven't got much to do.
    It's marvellous air in this part of the world;
    It can lengthen your life by several years.
    Remember what the Jostevale parson wrote:
    'People forget to die in this valley.'

BUTTONMOULDER. As far as the next cross-road; no further.

PEER. A priest, if I have to grab him with tongs!

                [He runs off.]

[*A heathery hillside. A path winds up over the hill.*]

PEER. This may be useful in lots of ways,
  Said Espen, picking up a magpie's wings.
  Who'd have thought my catalogue of sins
  Would extricate me on the last evening?
  But the situation is still very awkward;
  It's out of the frying pan into the fire.—
  But there's a well-tried proverb which says:
  While there is any life there's hope.

[*A* THIN PERSON *in a priest's cassock tucked up high, with a butterfly net over his shoulder, comes running along the hillside.*]

PEER. Who's this? A priest with a butterfly net!
  Hi-de-ho! I'm fortune's favourite!
  Good evening, Herr Pastor! It's a rough road—

THIN MAN. It is; but what wouldn't one do for a soul?

PEER. Aha! Then someone is heading for heaven?

THIN MAN. No; in a different direction, I hope.

PEER. May I go along with you for a bit?

THIN MAN. With pleasure; I'm always glad of company.

PEER. I've a weight on my mind—

THIN MAN.   Heraus! Fire ahead!

PEER. You see before you a decent man.
  I've strictly obeyed the country's laws;
  I've never been put in jug for anything;
  But sometimes you miss your footing and trip—

THIN MAN. Ah, yes; it happens to the best of us.

PEER. These trifles, you see—

THIN MAN.   Only trifles?

PEER.   Yes;
  I've always steered clear of sins *en gros*.

THIN MAN. In that case, dear man, leave me in peace.
  I'm not who you seem to think I am.

You observe my fingers? What do you think of them?

PEER. A most unusual output of nail.

THIN MAN. What now? You're looking down at my foot?

PEER [*pointing*]. Is that hoof natural?

THIN MAN.   I'm pleased to think so.

PEER [*raising his hat*]. I could have sworn you were a priest;
But I have the honour—. Well, best is best;
When the front door's open don't choose the back;
If the king's to be met with avoid the footman.

THIN MAN. Shake hands! You seem without prejudice.
Well, my dear, what can I do for you?
You mustn't ask me for power or wealth.
I couldn't supply them, not if you hanged me.
You wouldn't believe what a state trade is in.
The turn-over's almost non-existent;
No supply of souls; only once in a while
Some individual.—

PEER.   Have men so improved?

THIN MAN. On the contrary; sunk shamefully low.
They mostly end up in a casting-ladle.

PEER. Ah, yes—I've heard that ladle mentioned.
It's really the reason why I'm here.

THIN MAN. Speak your mind!

PEER.   If it isn't too much to ask,
I'd very much like—

THIN MAN.   A refuge? Is that it?

PEER. You have guessed my request before I made it.
You tell me business isn't flourishing,
So perhaps you won't be over-particular—

THIN MAN. But, my dear—

PEER.   My requirements aren't extravagant.
A salary isn't really necessary;
Just some sociability now and then.

THIN MAN. A heated room?

PEER.   Not too much heat;
  And I'd like a permit to leave again
  With no trouble—what they call 'no strings'—
  If a better position offers itself.

THIN MAN. Dear friend, I'm really extremely sorry,
  But you wouldn't believe how many requests
  Of a similar nature people send me
  When they have to wind up their earthly affairs.

PEER. But when I consider my past behaviour
  I know I have every qualification—

THIN MAN. You said it was trifling—

PEER.   Yes, in a sense;
  But I've just remembered I traded in slaves—

THIN MAN. There are men who have traded in wills and minds,
  But so stupidly they failed to get in.

PEER. I've shipped Brahman idols into China.

THIN MAN. Flim-flam! That just makes us laugh.
  People export much uglier images
  In sermons and art and literature,
  And we don't accept them.

PEER.   Maybe. But do you
  Know what?—I pretended to be a prophet!

THIN MAN. Abroad? Humbug! Most transcendentalists
  End up in the casting-ladle.
  If that's all you've got to back your claim
  I can't possibly house you, much as I'd like to.

PEER. But listen! In a shipwreck I clung to a boat—
  A drowning man grasps at a straw, you know;
  And every man for himself, as they say.
  I more or less robbed the cook of his life.

THIN MAN. I'd be just as pleased if you'd more or less
  Robbed a housemaid of something else.
  What is all this more-or-less palaver,

With due respect? Who do you think
Is going to waste expensive fuel
In times like these on such gutless nonentities?
Now, don't get upset; it's your sins I scoffed at;
And excuse me for not mincing matters.
Listen, my friend, put it out of your mind,
And get used to the thought of the casting-ladle.
What would you gain if I housed and fed you?
Think of it; you're a sensible man.
You'd still have your memory, yes, that's true;
But the view you would get down memory lane
Would be (to your heart, and mind as well)
What a Swede would describe as 'good bad fun'.
You've got nothing either to sob or smile about;
No cause for rejoicing or despair;
Nothing to chill or warm your blood;
Merely something to irritate you.

PEER. They say: It's not easy to find out where
Your shoes pinch when they're not on your feet.

THIN MAN. That's true. I have—Who's-it be praised—
No occasion to use more than one boot.
But how fortunate we mentioned boots;
It reminds me I've got to be on my way.
I've a joint to collect, a fat one, I hope.
I mustn't stand about gossiping.

PEER. And dare one ask what diet of sin
Put flesh on this fellow?

THIN MAN.   I rather gather
He has been himself, all his nights and days,
And that's what's important in the long run.

PEER. Himself? Do such people come under your aegis?

THIN MAN. It depends; at least the door's left open.
Don't forget there are two ways of being yourself;
The right and the wrong side of the garment.
You know that in Paris they've found the way
To make portraits with the help of the sun.
You can either show the straightforward picture

Or else what is called the negative.
In the latter light and shade are reversed;
To the unaccustomed eye it seems ugly;
But the likeness is in that, too, all the same;
It only needs to be brought out.
Now, if a soul has been photographed
During its life in the negative way,
The plate's not rejected because of that—
Quite simply, they hand it on to me.
And I subject it to further treatment,
And transform it by the accepted method.
I dampen, I plunge, I burn, I rinse
With sulphur and other ingredients,
Till the image emerges as held in the plate:
Namely, what's known as the positive.
But if someone like you half rubs himself out
Neither sulphur nor potash can help at all.

PEER. So you have to be as black as a crow
To be made as white as a snowy owl?
May I ask what name is on the plate
You're going to develop into a positive?

THIN MAN. It says Peter Gynt.

PEER.   Peter Gynt! I see!
And this Mr. Gynt is 'himself'?

THIN MAN.   So he says.

PEER. You'll find he's a very reliable man.

THIN MAN. Do you know him, then?

PEER.   Well, yes, in a way—
One knows so many.

THIN MAN.   I've not much time;
Where did you last come across him?

PEER.   Down
At the Cape.

THIN MAN. Di buona speranza?

OF GOOD HOPE?

PEER.   Yes,
  But he's off again soon, I understand.

THIN MAN. Then I must set off at once hot-foot.
  I only hope I'm in time to catch him!
  That Cape of Good Hope—I never liked it:
  Full of damned missionaries from Stavanger.

      [*He rushes off southwards.*]

PEER. The stupid hound! He's gone bounding off
  With his tongue hanging out. He'll find he's been conned!
  What a pleasure it was to pull his leg!
  Him, playing rich and lording it over me!
  What has he got to be cocky about?
  He won't get fat in his present business;
  He'll come off his perch with the whole bag of tricks.
  But I'm not too firm in the saddle myself
  Since I got the push, as you might say,
  From the self-owning aristocracy.

      [*A shooting-star is seen; he nods at it.*]

Greetings from Peer Gynt, brother meteor!
Sparkle, slip, and go into the dark—

    [*He clutches himself as though in terror, and goes deeper into the mist;
    he pauses, and then shouts:*]

Is there no one, no one on the swarming earth,
No one in hell, no one in heaven—!

    [*He reappears further down the road, throws his hat on the ground, and
    tears his hair. After a moment or two quiet descends on him.*]

So utterly destitute, a soul
Can return to nothing in the grey mist.
Excellent earth, don't be angry
That I trampled your grass to no purpose.
Excellent sun, you have thrown away
Your blessing of light on an empty shell.
No one was there to be warmed and ripened;
The owner, they tell me, was never at home.
Excellent sun, excellent earth.

You were fools to hold and shine on my mother.
The spirit is mean, and nature generous.
Life's a high price to pay for your birth.—
    I'll clamber up to the highest peak;
I would see the sun rise once again,
And stare at the promised land till I'm tired;
Then heap the snow over my head.
They can write above it: Here lies No one;
And afterwards—then—! Things must go as they will.

CHURCHGOERS [*singing on the forest path*].
        Blest morning,
       When God's might
  Spears earth with burning light:
      We, the inheritors,
    Sing out to heaven's towers
The Kingdom's battle-cry against the night.

PEER [*crouching in fear*].
Don't look that way! It's all a desert.
Alas, I was dead long before I died.

[*He tries to slink away through the bushes, but comes to the cross-road.*]

BUTTONMOULDER. Good-morning, Peer Gynt! Where's your list of
sins?

PEER. Don't you think I've been whistling and shouting
For all I'm worth?

BUTTONMOULDER.   And met with no one?

PEER. No one, except a strolling photographer.

BUTTONMOULDER. Well, the time's run out.

PEER.   Like everything else.
The owl smells its prey. Do you hear it hooting?

BUTTONMOULDER. It's the bell for matins.

PEER.   What's shining there?

BUTTONMOULDER. Just the light from a hut.

PEER.   And the sound I hear?

BUTTONMOULDER. Just a woman singing.

PEER.   That's where I'll find
The list of my sins—

BUTTONMOULDER [*catching hold of him*]. Set your house in order!

[*They have come out of the thicket and stand outside the hut. Dawn.*]

PEER. Set my house in order? It's there! Leave me!
If the ladle were as big as a coffin
It would still be too small for my sins and me!

BUTTONMOULDER. Till the third cross-road, then; but after that—!

[*He turns and goes.*]

PEER [*moving towards the hut*].
Forward or back, it's the same distance;
Out or in, it's equally narrow.

[*He stops.*]

No!—it's a wild, endless lament
To go in, go home, be back.

[*He takes a few steps, but stops again.*]

Round and about, said the Boyg! [*Hears a song in the hut.*]   No;
this time
Straight to it, however narrow the path is!

[*He runs towards the hut as* SOLVEIG *appears in the doorway, dressed
for church, a prayer-book wrapped in her handkerchief, a stick in her
hand. She stands there upright and gentle.*]

PEER [*throwing himself down on the threshold*].
Now condemn me, however you will!

SOLVEIG. He's here! He's here! God be praised!

[*She gropes for him.*]

PEER. Rate me with all the wrongs I have done!

SOLVEIG. You've done no wrong, my only boy!

[*She gropes again, and finds him.*]

BUTTONMOULDER [*behind the house*].
   The list, Peer Gynt?

PEER.   Cry out my guilt!

SOLVEIG [*sitting down beside him*].
   You made my life a cause for singing.
   Bless you, for coming back at last!
   And blessed our meeting at Whitsuntide!

PEER. I'm lost, then!

SOLVEIG.   There is one who leads.

PEER [*laughing*]. Lost! Unless you can answer a riddle!

SOLVEIG. Name it.

PEER.   Name it? All right, I will!
   Say where Peer Gynt has been all these years!

SOLVEIG. Been?

PEER.   With his destiny clearly marked
   As he first sprang from the mind of God!
   Can you tell me that? If not, homeward
   For me is down to the land of mists.

SOLVEIG [*smiling*]. It's an easy riddle.

PEER.   Then tell me the answer!
   Where was I myself, the entire, true man?
   Where did I have God's mark on my forehead?

SOLVEIG. In my faith, in my hope, and in my love.

PEER [*recoiling*]. What are you saying? Quiet! You're mocking me!
   You have mothered that thought of the man yourself.

SOLVEIG. Indeed, I did; but who is the father?
   He who forgives when the mother beseeches.

PEER [*a ray of light goes over him, and he cries out*].
   My mother; my wife; purest of women!
   Hide me there, hide me in your heart!

     [*He clings to her and hides his face in her lap. A long silence. The sun rises.*]

SOLVEIG [*singing softly*].

> Sleep, my boy, my precious dear.
> I will rock you, you my care.
>
> The boy has sat on his mother's knee
> All the day long the two at play.
>
> He has slept on his mother's breast
> All the day long. God give him rest.
>
> The boy has lain in my heart's eyrie
> All the day long. He is weary, weary.
>
> Sleep, my boy, my precious dear.
> I will rock you, you my care.

BUTTONMOULDER [*behind the house*].

> We shall meet at the last cross-road, Peer;
> And *then* we'll see whether—; I say no more.

SOLVEIG [*singing more loudly in the growing light*].

> I will rock you, you my care;
> Sleep, and dream, my home-returner.